What's Gone Wrong with Health Care?

Challenges for the new millennium

What's Gone Wrong with Health Care?

Challenges for the new millennium

Edited by Alison P Hill

Published by
King's Fund Publishing
11–13 Cavendish Square
London W1G 0AN

© King's Fund 2000

First published 2000

ISBN 1 85717 425 9

A CIP catalogue record for this book is available from the British Library

Available from:
King's Fund Bookshop
11–13 Cavendish Square
London
W1G 0AN

Tel: 020 7307 2591
Fax: 020 7307 2801

Printed and bound in Great Britain

Contents

Part 3
What should be done?

Foreword

The NHS is one of Britain's greatest political, economic and social achievements. A highly popular, efficient and equitable means of pooling the vast majority of the money we spend on health care into a single pot for individuals to draw on as and when they need it, regardless of ability to pay. Yet, that same system, by choice or by accident, is capable of extraordinary inhumanity.

The following book looks in depth at five examples of such inhumanity. It seeks to draw lessons for the whole health system from the experiences of five people, their families and their friends. It goes beyond the distant graphs and charts of medical research and management textbooks, to pull together knowledge based on the lived realities of health care as practised in Britain today. The questions raised by these five cases are fundamental to the future of the NHS. Putting to one side the stale arguments about whether the NHS, as it is presently designed, can and should survive, the book leads us to some radical conclusions about the future of health care.

First, it shows that a major power shift is needed, to give the people who use health services much more control over how they are treated. Reticent and confused as many patients may be, it is essential that the whole health system works to educate, to inform and to empower its users. It needs to offer genuine choices and make shared decision-making routine at all times, to overcome for once and for all the paternalism that still dominates much medical practice.

Second, it illustrates the importance of team working in health and social care. The current debate about the relative merits of a more responsive NHS, characterised by innovations like NHS Direct and walk-in centres, and a more traditional service with continuity of care provided by a single GP, needs to be moved on to another level. We need to think in terms of a health system where all the professionals involved in a person's care are listening to users, are talking to one another and are managed well as multidisciplinary teams. In a health system where care is delivered by such teams, continuity needs to be achieved by responsible communication and by at least one health professional ensuring that the whole team's work is co-ordinated around the stated needs of the patient.

Third, it makes painfully clear the fact that we have yet to resolve the dilemmas resulting from conflicts between the needs of individuals and the needs of their communities. Examples of such dilemmas in health include immunisations that have potentially damaging side effects, but which prevent disease spreading through the community; decisions about rationing expensive drugs and procedures; and the care of potentially dangerous people with serious mental illnesses. All raise questions about our thinking on medical ethics. Yet those questions are rarely discussed in the open, leaving hard-pushed health professionals to take tough choices in difficult circumstances with very little help.

Finally, it shows that, regardless of the technical wizardry that appears to characterise modern medicine, humanity is still the cornerstone of health care. Individual health professionals, educators, NHS organisations and policy-makers must never forget that caring for people – people experiencing pain, fear or anxiety – is their core business.

The future of health care in Britain is a major political issue. Rows about funding, about boundaries and about failings in the current system abound. It is absolutely crucial that, underpinning these debates, we have an understanding of how people experience health and health care, and that we aim at all times to improve the quality of that experience. The NHS stands for equality and humanity. It is essential that it lives by those values, for all the people who need it.

Rabbi Julia Neuberger
July 2000

Introduction

As the end of the 20th century approached, many policy-makers began to review recent history and to forecast or debate what should happen as the new millennium dawned. Health care was no exception. Our NHS was over 50 years old. It was widely thought that the principles on which it was founded were outdated. It was further being realised that improving people's health, while a legitimate public and government concern, is not purely the business of the health care system.

The Leeds Castle Foundation was one of many organisations to engage thinkers, policy-makers and the public in debate. The Foundation was set up in 1975 to preserve and maintain the historic and beautiful castle and its grounds near Maidstone in Kent. Lady Baillie, the last private owner of the castle, gave it to the nation for the public to enjoy and to be made available for international medical meetings and for the encouragement of the arts. Sir Roger Bannister is the medical trustee. In 1998 he approached Sir Cyril Chantler and the King's Fund, to put together a conference to consider the current and future challenges to health and health care.

The authors of this book were invited by Cyril Chantler to consider the issues. This book is drawn from our deliberations as we prepared for the conference. In dealing with our brief we confined ourselves to considering health care in the context of the NHS. We drew on our experience as workers in the NHS, as patients and observers of the service. We were concerned that in many ways the NHS is falling short of expectations. The increased demands on it come from demographic changes which have changed the focus from a service treating acute and largely infectious diseases to one that needs to address the burden of chronic disease and disability in an ageing population. Users of the service are becoming more aware of what health care can offer. The old 'doctor knows best' attitudes are being superseded by a less deferential, more critical perspective on what people would like the health service to do for them. Further pressure on the service, as a publicly funded system, comes from the increasing complexity and technical sophistication of available treatments.

We felt that we needed to change the question from 'what can be done' to 'what should be done?' We were anxious to ground our deliberations in the real world so we took as our starting point the stories of a number of people that were drawn from real life. These case histories make up Part 1 of this book, and were compiled with the help of other medical colleagues. Names and some details have been changed to preserve the privacy of these patients. We hope that some good will come out of telling these stories to a wider audience.

Part 2 consists of commentaries which each of us wrote from different perspectives. We are aware that many perspectives are missing. We offer them, as we did to the Leeds Castle conference, to stimulate debate and to encourage others to find solutions. We deliberately did not include discussions about resources. We assumed that resource for the NHS would stay broadly the same. There were two reasons for this. First, we wanted to get away from seeing the cure for the shortcomings of the NHS simply in terms of more money. We wanted to look beyond the funding issue, because we believe that criticism based solely on funding prevents critical and constructive thought about other aspects of providing health care. Second, we wanted our deliberations to get people in the service thinking about how they could change things themselves. The solution to the question of funding rests with the Government and its reaction to public demand.

During our preparation for the conference we were aware that our group was dominated by medical thinking. We were therefore keen to test our analyses on people from a wider range of backgrounds who attended the conference.

Part 3 consists of a summary of the deliberations of the conference in

October 1999. We are grateful to the Leeds Castle Foundation for allowing us to publish an extract from their report of the conference. It would have been easy for us to become idealistic and generalised, removed from the workaday world in this quiet and beautiful setting. But we tried to remain critical and above all practical, keenly conscious of what was going wrong and aware of what technical and social advance might make possible in the next 20 years or so.

Since we met, the Government has announced substantial extra funding for the NHS over the next three years. In return for a 'step-change' in funding the Prime Minister is demanding a step-change in attitude and behaviour from those responsible for modernising the NHS. As will be seen from this book, some of the changes we suggest can be brought about relatively simply and quickly, while others will take longer. Some will require the sensitive management of professional concerns and will need the commitment of those working in the service. In its overriding concern for performance management the Government should be aware of the negative effects that too much central monitoring and control can have on the morale and creativity of health professionals.

Those who work in the health service are not faced with this change process alone. The service needs to engage with those who use it. The public can provide ideas, fresh perspectives and support. They will need to be prepared and supported to play their new roles. The voluntary and private sectors have contributions to make. Some of the answers to our issues may come from individuals and organisations that have traditionally operated at some distance from health care.

As I write this, the Government is engaging groups of leaders from the health professions and from other national groups to think through an action plan for using this injection of funding. Many of the people who took part in the Leeds Castle conference are involved in this exercise. This gives us an unexpected opportunity to bring our suggestions to the notice of high-level policy-makers and to develop them further.

In publishing this book we hope to keep these issues in the view of politicians, people who work in the service and those who train and educate them, the voluntary sector and health related industries. We do not believe we have arrived at a definitive diagnosis of the health service's problems, nor at the ultimate prescription. But we believe we owe it to our patients, Ivy, John, Chris, Mary and Luke Warm Luke to learn from what happened to them, and to get things better for future users of the health service.

Alison P Hill
June 2000

Part 1

The case histories

Chapter 1

The uncomplaining Ivy Brown

Ivy was 57 when Frank, her husband, died. She had never had any very serious medical problems but over the past 15 years or so she had suffered from symptoms that affected her digestion and her bowels. Although she was sometimes quite disabled by the pain and socially embarrassed by a sudden urge to defecate, the senior partner, Dr Mason, didn't seem particularly interested in her problem and she suffered more or less in silence. He diagnosed spastic colon and treated her with intestinal sedatives.

A few weeks after Frank's death she was feeling low and isolated. She found herself worrying a great deal about her health. She decided to go and see her doctor about her worries. Dr Mason had retired and a new young doctor, Dr Wall, had joined the practice.

Is it serious?

Dr Wall listened attentively to her story. He told her that he thought she had irritable bowel syndrome (IBS) because she had had the symptoms for a long time. He told her that it was very common. He examined her thoroughly and told her that he could find no abnormalities, and her blood pressure was normal.

She told him, because he asked, that a couple of her uncles and a cousin had had cancer of the large bowel. Dr Wall thought it appropriate to check three faecal occult bloods to rule out cancer of her colon. He also ordered a full blood count and ESR* to check her general health.

---

*The Ethrocyte Sedimentation Rate (ESR) is a simple blood test commonly used to detect general ill health. If it is in the normal range, it provides good evidence that serious inflammatory disease, infection or widespread cancer is absent.

The tests showed that Ivy was not anaemic and that there was no blood in her stools. These results indicated to the doctor that there was nothing serious or dangerous going on. He explained to Ivy that there was no need for concern, and that her symptoms were probably due to some spasm in the muscles of the bowel, and that various foods and possibly stressful life events might influence these symptoms. There was certainly nothing to worry about, no sign of cancer and no likelihood of this ever turning into anything serious.

The locum

Two or three years elapsed before Ivy approached the practice again about her symptoms. She had visited the practice once or twice in the interim, seeing a different person each time. On one occasion she consulted about a painful toe and on another about some travel vaccinations linked to a planned holiday trip.

Then she had developed a sudden worsening of her abdominal symptoms while Dr Wall was away on holiday and she saw a locum, Dr Stone. Her pain was mainly in the upper abdomen and the possibility of acute peptic ulceration had occurred to him. The practice had a near-patient testing kit to test for Helicobacter serology and he found that she was Helicobacter-positive. This meant that there was a chance that her symptoms were due to peptic ulcer, although it may have been a coincidental phenomenon. Dr Stone decided to adopt a 'test and treat' strategy, prescribing a one-week course of triple therapy (a combination of anti-ulcer drugs and antibiotics) to eradicate the Helicobacter: a proton pump inhibitor, metronidazole and high-dose amoxycillin.

A few days later Ivy became very ill with abdominal pain, diarrhoea and rectal bleeding. She called out Dr Wall to visit her at home. He found her toxic and shocked with signs of peritonitis. He arranged her urgent admission to hospital. It seemed to him that Ivy had developed pseudo membranous colitis, a rare but potentially fatal complication of high-dose antibiotic therapy, associated in the scientific literature with Helicobacter eradication treatment.

Initially Ivy was treated with intravenous fluids and antibiotics, steroids and parenteral nutrition (intravenous feeding to bypass her failing digestive system), but these measures failed to settle her symptoms and the doctors went on to surgery to explore her bowel and to remove her colon. Ivy suffered a cardiac arrest during the operation and although she was successfully resuscitated, she developed a dense hemiplegia (a paralysis of one side of her body) in the post-operative period. When she was eventually taken off the ventilator, she was found to have lost her power of speech. A few days later, she developed a severe bronchopneumonia and required ventilation again. During all this time, the hospital staff did not contact Dr Wall, nor could he find out what was happening to Ivy when he tried.

The relatives

Ivy's daughter and son-in-law, a Florida lawyer, flew in to be with her during this severe illness. They found Ivy in an intensive care unit (ITU), on a respirator, fed intravenously, and with a bladder catheter and several intravenous lines in place. She was unable to communicate. During the first three or four days of their stay, two attempts to wean her off the ventilator were unsuccessful.

The consultant in charge of ITU explained that, at 62, paralysed and unable to speak, prolonged treatment was likely to do more harm than good, but the relatives felt that everything possible should be done for Ivy. As she developed multi-organ failure, this involved the institution of peritoneal dialysis, blood and plasma product transfusion and inotropic drugs to support her failing heart muscle.

Her relatives visited assiduously and took a close interest in the minutiae of Ivy's treatment, until 17 days later she died.

Chapter 2

Father John

John was a Catholic priest in his mid-70s. He began his working life as a barrister, having read law at Oxford. At the age of 24 he gave up law, breaking off his engagement to be married, and entered the Anglican Priesthood. He trained in an Anglo-Catholic Seminary and for many years worked as a missionary in the West Indies. On his return to the UK, he became a curate in an Anglican parish and eventually the vicar of a church in Derbyshire. He was an only child and after his father died, his mother came to live with him in the vicarage. It is likely that he would have entered the Catholic Church earlier than he did, but for family opposition. In his early 50s, after his mother died, he retrained in Rome as a Catholic priest before returning to take up a parish in London.

At the age of 70 he retired from his parish, but was looked after in a home for retired priests by a nursing order of religious sisters. He had no close relatives alive. He did, however, remain close to his godson, a doctor, and indeed had been a very close friend of the doctor's father.

Physical decline

In his late 60s, John became aware that his general health was deteriorating. Although fond of walking, he found that he could not walk as far or as fast as he used to because of breathlessness and he was generally lacking in energy. His GP, Dr Marks, referred him for a cardiologist's opinion, who found that he had early heart failure with widespread arteriosclerosis (an incurable degenerative condition, which can mean that blood circulation to vital tissues and organs can deteriorate). He had atrial fibrillation (an abnormality of heart rhythm, which can predispose to strokes) and mildly raised blood pressure, but these problems were well controlled with medication. His ankle swelling was controlled with diuretics, but it was explained to him that little could be done beyond this to improve his physical condition.

Over the next few years he had further problems. He suffered a series of cerebral ischaemic attacks (mini strokes), and he had trouble with his bladder caused by enlargement of the prostate gland, made more difficult by his diuretics. Arthritis affecting one hip further reduced his mobility and caused him constant pain. Most of the effective painkillers caused him unpleasant side effects or interfered with the medication controlling his heart failure. But his doctors did not think him fit enough for a hip replacement. In spite of his physical problems he remained mentally alert and had a small but close circle of friends.

At the age of 74 he suffered a sudden attack of severe chest pain. The nursing sisters in his retirement home were alarmed and called the general practitioner. His GP, Dr Marks, was off duty and an emergency doctor saw him. They diagnosed coronary thrombosis and arranged for his admission to a local teaching hospital. He was admitted to the geriatric ward. His godson was called, and explained to the consultant geriatrician under whom he had been admitted, John's medical and social history. With John's full consent it was decided that no active therapy should be given and he was discharged back to the retirement home. He realised that he was not going to get better and that the end of his life was approaching. He had a total commitment to his faith and he viewed the end of his life with equanimity.

A few weeks later a similar event occurred. Again, the emergency deputising service was called and a different doctor saw John and admitted him back to the same hospital. On this occasion, however, his condition was very much worse and he was admitted to the coronary care unit where he had a cardiac arrest. His godson was called and when he arrived he found that John had been resuscitated, was conscious, but severely distressed with breathlessness due to acute heart failure. He was treated with oxygen and an isosorbide drip to treat the heart failure. He was hardly able to communicate.

The sister in charge of the ward was unaware of the patient's previous medical condition or the decisions that had been made concerning future care. The team had of course acted in good faith in treating the cardiac arrest and delighted that, as they saw it, the treatment had been successful. The godson saw the consultant in charge, explained the circumstances and requested that aggressive treatment should be discontinued and morphine given instead to relieve John's distress. While understanding and accepting the explanation, the clinical team were loath to withdraw active therapy and it was sometime before it was agreed that morphine should be given. In spite of this the isosorbide drip and the oxygen therapy were continued.

However, after 48 hours it was acknowledged that treatment was not going to be successful. John was moved to a side room and active treatment discontinued. By this time he was unconscious with irregular breathing. A curious event occurred about 24 hours after this when John suddenly woke up, sat up and said to his godson, 'something has gone wrong with the chronology of this'. His godson reassured him that 'everything was under control' and John said 'thank you', lay back and sank into a coma. He died 24 hours later with the nursing sisters at his bedside.

Chapter 3

Mary Fisher's bewildering experiences

Mary is 70 years old. Her husband died several years ago and was in the Army. She has five children: three sons and two daughters. Her sons are married with families and live some distance away. Her youngest daughter, Heather, is aged 32. Mary has lived in a council house for 20 years and has lived in 30 different houses during her lifetime. This meant frequent moves to different localities to accommodate her husband's job. She had learned to be adaptable and self-reliant.

Health problems

Ten years ago she began experiencing hospital care. First, she needed a heart operation and then four years later she broke her leg. Three years ago she had increasing difficulty getting about because her damaged leg was stiff. She had a bad fall that took her into casualty and shortly after that she had a hip replacement. Everything seemed to go very well at first. The hospital team were pleased with her and she was discharged quickly, but at home she found things difficult. She was not confident getting about in her flat and spent most of the day sitting down waiting for the fleeting visits of her home carer. After a couple of weeks she became ill. She developed chest pain and breathlessness. At ten o'clock one night, her GP, Dr Block, sent her back to hospital with a suspected thrombosis on her lung and pneumonia. She was found to have a deep vein thrombosis in her leg that was probably a complication of her immobility after surgery and caused her other problems.

Stranded

While in hospital she felt bewildered by the big mixed ward. She felt sorry for the nursing staff who always seemed stretched, always rushing about, struggling to cope. The nurse who had admitted her had been attentive and caring, but she never saw her again. Staff always seemed to be changing. Mary wondered what was to become of her. She did not really understand what was wrong. She liked the doctors, especially the young one, but she didn't like to bother them with so many questions. She thought they would think her silly and she knew they were very busy looking after really sick patients.

After only five days, when she was still feeling wretched and too weak to walk, it was decided that she was well enough to go home. A porter took her in a wheel chair to the front entrance and parked her near the reception desk to wait for her transport. She sat there for two hours. No one approached her. Eventually a taxi turned up for her. The taxi driver was amazed to find her in a wheel chair. He said he could not take her because she could not walk out to the taxi. He went away. Eventually Heather phoned up to see why her mother had not arrived at home. She phoned the ward and a nurse went down to reception to find Mary stranded. Afterwards Mary said she could see the funny side of it. But at the time, stuck in that draughty place with everyone ignoring her, she felt bewildered and uncared-for.

At home again she did not improve. She still spent most of the day sitting down. She returned to out-patients where she was kept waiting for hours. No one took the trouble to tell her what to expect. When she was given her next appointment she was told to attend another hospital which she did not know. No one explained why.

At home things went from bad to worse. She could not get out of her flat because she lived on the fourth floor and there was no working lift as it was often vandalised and not repaired. She was lonely and low and was not feeding herself. Food from meals on wheels was left untouched. She was worried because she felt so ill. She asked Diane, the district nurse, why she felt so ill, why she was unsteady on her feet and when she was going to get better. Diane did not know and said she would ask Dr Block to call. Dr Block came a week later and decided to refer her to a day hospital in an attempt to improve her mobility and her motivation to care for herself.

Cared for at last

Mary did not know what to expect from the day hospital and was reluctant to go. But after she had been attending three days a week for a few weeks she found, like the other patients, that she had got to know the staff and looked forward to her visits. She noticed that her companions did not want to be discharged and she could understand why. She dreaded having to go back to endless days in her lonely flat.

Chapter 4

Chris Adams – the high price of confusion

A rare complaint

When Chris Adams was in his 30s, he developed an autoimmune disease (a condition in which the body becomes allergic to itself), which was successfully treated and controlled. He worked as secondary school teacher. When he was 45, things suddenly got worse. By then he had three young children.

On his way to work he suffered a severe nosebleed which would not stop. As a result he went to the local A&E department. A blood test showed that one of his clotting proteins was absent. Further tests made it clear that he had developed a bleeding tendency, which was diagnosed as acquired haemophilia, secondary to an autoimmune condition. Following the nosebleed, Chris's first catastrophe was an injury to his knee, and Chris bled into his knee so severely that he required a blood transfusion.

During the next year he had several episodes of severe bleeding into his joints, such that he needed blood transfusions and also treatment with Factor VIII (a blood clotting factor) to stop his bleeding.

Things get worse

However, it soon became apparent that he was developing antibodies to this Factor VIII and required a very expensive artificially engineered form of this drug called Recombinant Factor VIIa. It was estimated that if Chris continued to have the same number of joint bleeds, the total cost of treatment in the next year could amount to

£500,000 to £1 million. A request was made to the health authority for provision of this Factor VIIa to be used when he had bleeds.

Sadly for Chris, he began to go yellow and developed jaundice. Over the next six months it was clear that his liver function tests (LFTs) were deteriorating. He was referred to a local liver unit where he was diagnosed as having primary biliary cirrhosis secondary to his autoimmune condition.

Over the next six months, Chris's biliary cirrhosis worsened, causing vitamin K deficiency which further exacerbated his bleeding tendency. It was clear that this would endanger Chris's life. The only way to treat this was with a liver transplant, although there was a chance that the biliary cirrhosis might develop again in his new liver.

Chris and his wife realised that he would die without further treatment. There was no question in their minds that the health service should fund this and although they understood that there was a considerable risk attached to having a liver transplant on top of Chris's other problems, Chris was desperate to survive for his family's sake and he would try anything.

The health authority's dilemma

At this time the health authority, which would have to cover the costs of Chris's case, was heading for an overspend of between £18–£27 million on a total budget of £600 million. To control the situation it was cutting services available to the population (750,000) it served – a population that was among the most deprived in the country. Already many treatments that were provided for the public elsewhere were not available to this health authority's residents, such as varicose vein operations, and some drugs like beta interferon for multiple sclerosis. Surgeons were laid-off and any elderly resident needing a hip or knee replacement would have to wait a very long time, even though the authority's hip and knee replacement rates were among the lowest in the country. It was against this backdrop that the authority had to decide whether to allocate nearly £1 million for the treatment of one patient, Chris Adams.

The authority was faced with a further request not only to fund Chris's Recombinant Factor VIIa but also to fund a liver transplant, the success or otherwise of which was not known. In order to take such a decision the authority set up an elaborate procedure. This involved an assessment of the evidence as to the likelihood that a transplant would benefit the patient, taking note of the patients' views, of the family's views, and of the diagnosis. It also assessed the likely prognosis given that Chris not only suffered from cirrhosis requiring a transplant but had also acquired haemophilia, which would greatly add to his chance of dying during or following surgery. His chances could be described as slender at best.

The arguments were presented as a choice between, first, possibly saving one patient's life at a cost of approximately £1 million but with little strong evidence that the treatment would be successful and, second, doing for instance 100 hip replacements for other people in the area. Lawyers advised that the only defensible decision was taken – that is, to say yes to providing treatment for the individual. Not enough detail was known about where the rest of the NHS resources were going and who would be benefited or not.

Precipitate action

While the health authority discussed the likelihood that a liver transplant would benefit Chris, the doctors felt that their hands were forced when Chris went into acute liver failure and a compatible liver was suddenly available. Such an opportunity was unlikely to happen again and they had to move quickly. A few hours' delay might destroy the liver. They took the view that saving Chris's life was more important than delaying further by arguing over money.

Chris seemed to make a good recovery initially. He was feeling quite well, despite the large number of drugs he was required to take, and he was still taking his recombinant factor VIIa. Sadly, however, he began to reject the transplanted organ and no treatment could be found to control the rejection adequately. He began to bleed and develop further complications and died three months after the transplant.

Chapter 5

Luke Warm Luke – a calamity of mental ill health

An unhappy and difficult youth

Michael – who later changed his name to Luke Warm Luke – was born in south London in 1962, the fifth of eight children. His parents were originally from the West Indies. Around the time of leaving school at 16 he was convicted of rape on school premises after hours and also convicted twice of being a 'suspected person' because of loitering with intent to steal. He spent ten months in borstal having been assessed in Wormwood Scrubs as having fair intelligence but a poor educational standard. At borstal, he obtained a C-grade in a course on painting and decorating.

After leaving borstal he worked as a restaurant assistant for a few months. He was fined for obstructing police officers when the police searched his girlfriend, and he spent three months in prison for attempting to steal a purse in Brixton Road. His probation officer reported Michael's 'bitterness and unhappiness about (a) the country he lives in and (b) the situation he finds himself in'.

The recognition of mental illness

When Michael was 20, the family GP referred him to the psychiatric services for the first time. He was immobile with what was thought to be schizophrenia or depression, and was admitted under the Mental Health Act. In hospital he was described as isolated, unpredictable and withdrawn, and he was not happy about taking medication. He was readmitted several times with aggressive and violent behaviour, once having resisted the attempts of eight policeman, two ambulance drivers, his parents and a psychiatrist to get him out of his room at home. He took various prescribed drugs reluctantly. His family did not want him back at home so he was referred to the Homeless Single Persons Team and obtained council housing. He went to out-patients a few times and said that he had decided to stop taking his tablets.

Treatment difficulties

From 1983 to 1985 Michael's schizophrenia recurred when he stopped his oral medication. In 1986 the Inner London Crown Court made a hospital order under the Mental Health Act following an episode in which Michael attacked and wounded several people with a knife in the street in Brixton. While in Brixton Prison he was given chlorpromazine and showed some Parkinsonian side effects.

A few months after being admitted he was feeling very cooped up and restricted in the secure ward. At this stage, Michael changed his name to Luke (Luke Warm Luke in full), which he said was his name according to the Bible. He continued to be displeased by the side effects of his treatment but because the staff thought he was more relaxed and sociable with treatment, depot medication was considered. Before it began he assaulted several patients and absconded from hospital.

Within a few weeks he was arrested for the robbery of a taxi driver at knifepoint. A forensic psychiatrist described him as an extremely dangerous man. He was convicted of the robbery and committed to hospital where he remained for three years on depot medication.

Apparent improvement

In 1990 Luke was transferred back to a medium secure psychiatric unit in London. He felt well and did not want to continue medication. After about six months his depot medication was discontinued and he received no medication for more than six months. But he was then restarted on oral medication because of a relapse of violent and aggressive behaviour. A period of stability followed and in January 1992 a Mental Health Tribunal agreed to his discharge conditional on him accepting medication as directed. He was still complaining about his treatment and its side effects. He went to live at a hostel and began a training course.

In May 1992 the consultant 'reluctantly agreed to make arrangements for discontinuing the medication' because of Luke's persistent objections and the consultant's view that the medication was not enforceable in the community. The consultant's opinion was that in managing a difficult patient like Luke Warm Luke a therapeutic alliance was necessary and a good working relationship of trust was paramount. In the following months Luke missed several out-patient appointments but he was seen by different members of the team (consultant, community psychiatric nurse, and social worker) who occasionally discussed him by telephone. There was concern among some of the team members that he was deteriorating.

Out of control

In January 1993 Luke seriously assaulted a security guard at a London Electricity Board depot because the guard would not recharge his electricity keys. A second guard described the assailant and Luke was arrested at the site after a severe struggle. The injured guard was not lawfully in the UK and wished to have nothing to do with the courts. The police decided that no charge would be brought, and released Luke from custody after a forensic medical examiner (who had no knowledge of Luke or medical reports) did not take the view that Luke was mentally ill. Luke made his own way to the psychiatric emergency clinic. The consultant was contacted but Luke decided to leave and was not detained. He was finally detained and admitted two days later, much more ill than before.

Luke was conditionally discharged after six months after similar progress and in similar circumstances to his previous admission. He missed several out-patient visits, and there were staff changes and no team meetings during that time.

Fatal freedom

At the beginning of October 1994, Luke Warm Luke went to the psychiatric emergency clinic asking to see the consultant. He was more agitated than staff had seen him before and the consultant who was working in another hospital that day asked for him to be kept there. However, Luke left and was not detained. It was arranged that the community psychiatric nurse, accompanied by a male colleague for security, would visit Luke the next day. Very late that night a woman friend visited Luke and neighbours heard her persuade him to open the door to her despite his initial unwillingness. Neighbours heard a struggle and when an ambulance was called the woman visitor was found outside the house with multiple stab wounds. She died shortly afterwards.

Luke Warm Luke was arrested, charged and convicted of manslaughter. He is now detained for treatment at Broadmoor without limit of time. A subsequent public enquiry questioned aspects of Luke's management, especially communication within the team undertaking his care, and whether the chances of his relapse when taking charge of his own treatment had been sufficiently appreciated. The enquiry also commented at length about the detailed working of the Mental Health Act. There have been wide differences of opinion among the senior medical and managerial staff involved as to the quality of the care and assessment of risk in this sad case.

Part 2

The commentaries

Chapter 6

From the patient's perspective

Alison P Hill

When we are sick

When someone becomes ill they need to make sense of what is happening to them. They approach health professionals for explanation and help. The traditional view of a patient is of one who is dependent on the wisdom and expertise of the clinician providing health care. But the growth of notions of therapeutic partnerships and the wider distribution and understanding of medical scientific knowledge, challenge the status of health care professionals and mean that this traditional view is called into question.

Research shows us again and again that patients want to be taken seriously: their suffering, their concerns and their views. For every person who becomes ill, that experience and its meaning are unique. They want to know what is wrong – to have a name for their affliction, to know that they are not alone, what can be done to help and what is likely to happen to them. They want to be able to explain to family, friends and employers about their illness, to have their affliction validated, so that these people too can understand and support them. A patient, particularly with a long-term illness, needs to be 'recognised, appreciated and understood.'[1]

Patients also want to be treated humanely and with respect. The relationship between patient and therapist is of crucial importance in the healing process. The quality of that relationship has a strong bearing on trust, confidence and compliance (that is concordance between the doctor's preferred course of action and the patient's behaviour), and on the patient's tolerance of adverse events and uncertainty. It may also contribute to the extent to which patients feel empowered to deal with their own illnesses.

Objectivity and experience

There has been an increasing dichotomy between rational science and lived experience that dates from the Enlightenment (18th century). Medical science sits uneasily between rationality and emotion. Aspiring more towards rationality, it increasingly tries to embrace the stringent requirements of scientific rigour and a detached generalised view of reality. Patients usually welcome the categorisation of their illness as a disease because this often brings with it hope of a cure, or at least improvement. But they also need to understand their illness in their own terms, integrating it with their emotional response to their experience and using their own semantic or explanatory frameworks. Their views and concerns are better served by observational rather than empirical study.

There is increasing evidence that many patients want to play a larger role in making decisions about the management of their medical condition. With increasing options, it becomes more and more important that patients are given the information and the skills to distinguish between them and to exercise their preferences. Patient preferences for treatment and outcome are individually based and clinicians need the skills and organisational support to be able to understand and work with these. There is evidence that where patients exercise their preferences in choosing treatment, they are more satisfied and the health outcomes are improved.[2]

For nearly two decades, there have been strong cases made from many quarters for changing the model of interaction between patient and doctor to a more patient-centred approach.[3,4,5] There is much current interest, at least among clinical researchers and teachers, in the patient's perspective, in their accounts and their understanding of their illness. But this is much less apparent in current practice. And there is even less real progress towards a shared model of clinical decision-making. All of the case studies show examples of patients having their preferences ignored (Father John), being unable to be heard (Ivy Brown and Luke Warm Luke) or to understand what is going on (Chris Adams and Mary Fisher). Although the circumstances and outcomes for each of these patients are particularly striking, the problems they demonstrate with communication between the world of the patient and that of the health professional are commonplace.

Ivy Brown

It is difficult to know what Ivy had wanted from her doctor. She seems to have felt that with Dr Mason she was not attended to and that her suffering was not taken seriously. It is likely that, through deference perhaps, or because she could not find the best words, she was unable to communicate her distress to the doctor and gave up trying. Would she nowadays have consulted magazines, neighbours, or the Internet for experiences of other patients? Would her relatives and friends have helped her find it? Would she then have been able to be more specific about her concerns, needs and preferences? What would the reaction of her doctor been?

Young Dr Wall seems to have taken things more seriously in that he ordered investigations and took some trouble to reassure Ivy. It may be that the tests and their results reassured Ivy, but Dr Wall's actions may have heightened her anxiety and increased her confusion. It is more likely that Dr Wall's actions were aimed at, and only effective in, reassuring himself.

When Dr Stone prescribed for her suspected peptic ulcer, we do not know how much choice Ivy was given on treatment at that stage, or how much she understood the risks and benefits of the various options. It would have been necessary to have some way of allowing her to understand and evaluate the situation and the doctor may not have had the skills or the time, assuming that Ivy did not have the capacity to consider the options. Doctors often ignore the fact that patients are people who handle conflicting priorities, complex information and difficult decisions in other domains of their lives. If she had been given more information about the potential side effects of the treatment she is unlikely to have persisted with it as long as she did, and maybe the consequences would not have been so dire.

Father John

Father John also seems to have been the victim of patronising attitudes. Once he had made a decision about how he wanted his last illness to be managed and gained the agreement of his doctors, why were his wishes ignored? It may simply have been that his wishes were not widely enough known, or that real agreement had not been reached with key people such as the nursing sisters or his GP. Or it might have been that the wishes of this mild man were not taken seriously enough by those in whose power their implementation lay.

Why was it necessary for someone other than Father John himself to negotiate with the geriatrician for non-intervention? People are vulnerable when they are sick and often do not want to take explicit responsibility for significant decisions about their treatment. In one sense when patients are so sick, unequal power relationships between patient and clinician in which the doctor is dominant are no bad thing. By definition any caring relationship is unequal in terms of power. But assumptions are often made about what patients wish for themselves or want to relinquish, and being dependent they do not like to complain.

Mary Fisher

Mary's story is based on her own account. It illustrates the phenomenon of dissatisfaction expressed in the light of apparent satisfaction with the health service. Most questionnaire surveys reveal high levels of satisfaction whereas detailed narratives often reveal negative experiences that are often far from trivial. One explanation is that general sentiments of gratitude for the National Health Service are related to fairly low expectations of it. Younger people and those educated at a higher level are less likely to be deferential to clinical staff, and more consumerist in their views on health care.

There is a widespread tendency for staff to objectify patients, and not to consider their personhood. The behaviour of the helpdesk receptionist in ignoring Mary's plight when she was stranded on the way home appears heartless and rude. She might argue that she could not take particular care of Mary, and that it was not her job to note that she was stranded and to communicate with the ward (she might not know where Mary had come from) or with her family. Mary, on the other hand, may have thought that the helpdesk was part of the hospital bureaucracy, that the young woman represented officialdom, and would therefore be able to see that things were wrong and could put them right. Mary was also in an alien environment and further disempowered by being in a wheel chair. Therefore she probably did not have the courage to take the initiative herself.

Both Mary and Ivy illustrate the deference of people – particularly older people – which prevents them asking doctors questions sufficient to clarify things for them, or to satisfy their curiosity. They are therefore seen as much more passive than in fact they are. They will often give up when they perceive themselves unable to impart their experiences or preferences to doctors because of inability to find the words that will engage the doctor's interest. This sort of problem can be magnified by hearing and speech difficulties, which are also more common among older people.

Although older people appear to want to rely on the doctor's judgement, to be more uncomplaining and passive than younger people, they express concern when subjected to inhumane or patronising behaviour. Because they suffer in deference does not mean that they would not like things to be different. The need to 'modernise' therapeutic relationships and to bring behaviour in the world of health care closer to society's expectations in other domains is a concern for all groups, although not always clearly articulated.

These patients' stories suggest seven key questions for bringing health care up-to-date from the patients' perspective:

How can the patient's perspective be better integrated into routine health care?

Where health care is provided by the state out of public funds, the public wants to be assured that its money is being spent wisely and to good effect. Individuals will have a view on the quality of care they receive, although their expectations of the NHS as a publicly-funded system may be low. But the individual patient can find a bureaucratised health service alienating, confusing and uncaring. It is difficult to get them to express their opinions in a constructive way. Much then rests on the health professionals working in such a system, who need to engage highly-refined clinical and social skills to provide care that is acceptable, humane and accessible within available resources.

How can patients be empowered and doctors prepared for a more patient-centred approach?

Because patients tend to be deferential to doctors it is often difficult for them to have their concerns dealt with and their preferences taken into account. Most health professionals are motivated by an altruistic approach to caring for patients. However, they are finding increasing difficulty in employing the traditional model in which they have been trained because it is becoming outdated in a society which increasingly challenges the paternalistic stance and hegemonic approach to medical knowledge of the profession. Conversely, lack of skills and time (they say) prevents them from practising in a more patient-centred way.[6]

Other caring professions are perhaps less handicapped by such a traditionalist approach but have their own historically determined behaviours that make for difficult inter-professional relationships. The organisation of care and treatment is becoming increasingly complex. As the number of clinicians who will deal with any patient also increases, there is more opportunity for poor communication. Patients find multiple approaches confusing and inconsistent. Patients need to know what is going on and what they can and should expect. They need to know what questions to ask, and how to do this without fear of alienating the staff on whose goodwill they depend.

'Integrated care pathways' are a method of service delivery which seem to offer complex services focused on the needs of individual patients and allow the patient's journey to be tracked and audited. The framework is based as far as possible on evidence of effectiveness, and any deviations in what happens to the patient have to be accounted for and recorded. They may offer a way of explaining to patients the roles of the different people and service departments with which they come into contact, give patients a record of their progress and give them prompts for asking questions about their treatment. More often, they are a vehicle for division of labour between health professionals that is in their own interests. There is no evidence that the care pathway approach gives patients any more choice, control or information about their treatment than any other way of organising care.

Studies of patients' views on the quality of care in general practice show that doctors' interpersonal and technical skills are often more important to patients than issues of access, availability and service provision.[7]

Theoretical models have been derived for looking at therapeutic encounters in medicine, and for teaching consultation skills, but current research is still demonstrating little movement towards more patient-centred models of care. Theories of why there is so little change range from the sociological (doctors as professionals would naturally not wish to relinquish power) to the psychological (any one who has high ideals of personal behaviour and who feels themselves to be criticised will seek to blame someone or something else).

Models explaining resistance to change demonstrate the complex and context sensitive nature of behavioural change.

If doctors and other clinicians are to change their behaviour and attitudes to patients and the management of their illnesses, patients may have to change too. If ways could be found to make more explicit to patients the role they play in decisions about their health care, then a powerful contextual driver might appear. If clinical practice guidelines based on robust evidence of effectiveness acceptable to patients were made available to them, what would be the effect on therapeutic relationships and on the outcomes of care? If doctors are confident in their role and the contribution they have to make, they are more open to a patient-centred mode of practice.

In what ways can patients contribute to the preparation of clinicians for this change in role?

Patients have for a long time played an important role in the training of undergraduates. But they are often 'passive' participants, used only to tell their story, and consent to examination or the student's practice of techniques. Thoughtful clinicians and some undergraduates will naturally learn from spending time understanding the patients' experience and tapping into their expertise. More needs to be done to make this learning habit universal among clinicians. Increasingly patients play a role in giving feedback on the student's performance, and are occasionally, when used in examinations, asked their opinion, although they do not (in the UK at present) act as examiners and give marks.

In The Netherlands, women have been recruited and trained as teachers to guide undergraduates learning to carry out intimate examinations. These are not 'patients' as there is no therapeutic relationship between the tutor and the student or even with the institution in which the teaching takes place.

Patients, and simulated patients, are also being used as both exemplar cases and as tutors in continuing postgraduate education. Perhaps the crucial contribution will be made when patients can contribute to curriculum planning and setting standards for qualifying examinations.

How can treatment be delivered in a more supportive and humane way?

The ultimate test for a health professional is to ask what behaviour they would like for themselves or their relatives. It is often when they experience NHS care for themselves or for their close relatives that they realise its shortcomings. Putting themselves in the patients' shoes does not mean assuming that their preferences or concerns would be those of the patient, but offers an attached and critical way of assessing their behaviour in terms of notions like caring, being respectful and attentive. Traditional medical training emphasises that doctors should be detached and tends to make doctors defensive rather than reflective and aware of their effects on others.

Where patient competence is affected, who can and should be the advocate for the patient?

In several of the case studies, patients were unconscious or uncommunicative when crucial decisions had to be made about their care. Luke Warm Luke's case is particularly powerful, as it points up the particular difficulties with mentally ill people whose competence may fluctuate and may not be as it seems. When he was ill and he presented for treatment, staff did not help him to stay to access it. When he seemed well and able to stay on treatment, insufficient account was taken of what might happen if he followed his own inclination to give up medication, because he was unable to foresee the consequences for himself.

With increasing emphasis on patients' autonomy, the position of those people with compromised ability to think things through and make choices is even more poignant. The important point seems to be that people acting on behalf of others should do what they believe that person would wish and what seems morally right. Clinicians should be aware of their power and their fiduciary responsibilities but should be discouraged from taking decisions without consulting others both independent of and attached to the patient. It is unlikely that any one person can speak in the best interests of an incompetent patient. Yet decisions have to be made that are felt to be moral and that society can support. A kind of reflective altruism is called for. Priscilla Alderson studied what she termed 'proxy consent' in a paediatric cardiac surgery unit. She saw consent to treatment as a 'process through which families and doctors arrive at medical and moral agreement that satisfied both parties'.[8]

What effect will technological advances have on patients' attitude to accessing health care?

Not only is technical advance making complex treatment available, and making serious conditions amenable to effective treatment, it is also moving the boundary of health care more into the domain of everyday life. Drugs such as Viagra, treatments for obesity, and hormone replacement therapy may need to remain available only through the offices of qualified professionals, but relatively safe therapeutic agents may become more directly available to the public. Currently medication available over the counter (OTC) is aimed at the relief of symptoms, doses are small and packages contain only a few days' supply. Research shows that people rarely persist with OTC medication long enough for it to effectively cure a condition (H2 antagonists for dyspepsia, for example). Continuing with a course of treatment until after troublesome symptoms have disappeared to ensure the successful treatment of the underlying treatment is part of the ethos of effective medical care, and often requires continual encouragement by professionals. Viagra and the new anti-flu drug Relenza are designed to treat common conditions, which may not hitherto have needed medical recognition and a diagnostic label. Media interest in such technical advances will encourage people to access health care if it is perceived that this is the only way they can benefit from these advances. The public not only needs to know of new treatments, but also how effective they are and how to find them before they will significantly increase the numbers of people wanting to access the health service.

Other technical advances are designed to reduce the need for patients to access the health service. Over the counter diagnostic aids, such as pregnancy tests, and near-patient testing such as blood glucose monitoring equipment, only reduce access when patients can handle the technology in a way that gives reliable results. These aids must be acceptable for self-administration (unlike the toilet-paper test for rectal bleeding), cheap and both doctors and patients must trust the results.

Notwithstanding these provisos, near-patient and over the counter testing will alter the degree to which patients can investigate things for themselves and may reduce the risks and inconvenience of invasive tests. Advances in telemedicine may make it easier to perform high-tech investigations and to gain specialist opinions without sending the patient to hospital, thereby keeping them closer to their own familiar world.

What differences will technological advances make to shared decision-making?

Advancing technology in the management of information means that the doctor is not the only source of medical technological knowledge, but that information packages can take the patient through a complex process of accessing and processing information and making judgements. For patients who choose to use these, and where they are available, doctors may not have to spend precious consulting time trying to impart the information, but could spend the time more profitably discussing matters and reaching a decision that meets the concerns of both parties. Time will always be limited in the NHS and using technical aids to allow patients to enter the decision-making process as equal players could help. But at present many health professionals are suspicious of these programmes, and prefer to be the source of medical information on which they hope decisions will be made. Patients have always gleaned information and advice from many sources, but doctors have imagined that it is their sole responsibility to decide how much a patient should be told. This position is increasingly untenable but leaves doctors wondering about their future role in therapeutic relationships.

Conclusion

People value health care that is attentive, respectful and personal. The challenges are for health services to be able to provide such services despite other bureaucratic and political imperatives, and for health professionals and patients to change the nature of therapeutic relationships.

References

1. Toombs SK. *The Meaning of Illness. A phenomenological account of the different perspectives of physician and patient.* Dordrecht: Kluwer Academic Publishers, 1992.

2. Brody DS, Miller SM, Lerman C and Smith MD. Patient perception of involvement in medical care: relationship between illness attitude and outcomes. *J.Gen. Int. Med.* 1989; 4: 506–11.

3. Waitzkin H. Doctor-patient communication: Clinical implications of social scientific research. *JAMA* 1984; 252: 2441–46.

4. Tuckett D, Boulton M, Olson C and Williams A. *Meetings between experts: An approach to sharing ideas in medical consultations.* London: Tavistock Publications, 1985.

5. Stewart M *et al. Patient-centred medicine: transforming the clinical method.* Thousand Oaks: Sage, 1996.

6. Elwyn G, Edwards A and Kinnersley P. Shared decision-making in primary care: the neglected second half of the consultation. *BJGP* 1999; 49: 477–82.

7. Rees Lewis J. Patient views on quality care in general practice: literature review. *Soc. Sci. Med.* 1994; 39: 655–70.

8. Alderson P. *Choosing for children. Parents consent to surgery.* Oxford: OUP, 1990.

Chapter 7

The duties of care and the values of medicine in the new millennium

Len Doyal

The discussion at Leeds Castle was about the values which should inform the practice of medicine in the new millennium and the related question of how health care should be organised within the NHS in order to meet the needs of both individual patients and of society. In the paper that follows, I will initially outline the moral and professional boundaries within which the practice of good medicine should occur, particularly focusing on the duties of care and some of the difficulties of interpreting them in practice. The conclusions of this discussion will then be applied to a range of cases based on true circumstances. Among other things, these cases illustrate the ethico-legal dilemmas which health care professionals will increasingly have to face and resolve in the forthcoming years.

The duties of care in theory and practice

Good ethical practice in medicine must be understood against the background of the accepted duties of clinical care.

What are the duties of care and why?

On the face of it, there is a formidable professional consensus about the substance of the duties of care. Three duties are of particular importance. Using their expertise to an acceptable standard, clinicians should:

- protect the life and health of their patients

- respect the autonomy of their patients

- carry out the first two duties with fairness and justice.

A common way of stating the first duty is that clinicians should act in the best interests of their patients, accepting that there will be circumstances when not providing specific types of treatments – including those which are life-saving – may be justified in these terms. In clinical practice, the second duty reduces to obtaining the informed consent of patients and to respecting their confidentiality. The third duty places moral priority on respect for equality, stressing that the first two duties should be exercised in the same way toward all individuals and that prejudice should not diminish the quality of care.

Each of these duties gains wide-ranging support within the professional and regulatory literature. Perhaps the most important illustrations are from The General Medical Council's *Duties of a Doctor*:

1. *First duty of care: You must take suitable and prompt action when necessary ... [including] an adequate assessment of the patient's condition ... providing or arranging investigations or treatments when necessary ... and referring the patient to another practitioner, when indicated.*

2. *Second duty of care: To establish and maintain trust you must [among others] listen to patients and respect their views ... respect the right of patients to be fully involved in decisions about their care ... [including the right] to refuse treatment or to take part in teaching or research ... [and] not pass on any personal information which you learn in the course of your professional duties, unless [patients] agree.*

3. *Third duty of care: You must not allow your view about a patient's lifestyle, culture, beliefs, race, colour, sex, sexuality,*

age, social status, or perceived economic worth to prejudice the treatment you give or arrange.

Similar statements can be found in guidance published by the British Medical Association, the medical and surgical Royal Colleges and the Defence Associations.

Of course, it will take more to defend the moral standing of the three duties of care than the existence of this professional consensus. Three philosophical arguments are usually used for this purpose, either separately or together. The first emphasises the importance of trust in clinical relationships with patients, noting that successful medicine would be impossible without it. The duties of care are justified because without them there would be a breakdown in trust and a significant reduction of the benefit which successful medicine provides. The second argument emphasises the importance of individual autonomy in understanding what gives humans their moral status within the animal kingdom. Here, the key question is how to ensure that doctors will treat patients with the particular type of respect that their human dignity demands. To the degree that it is accepted that we are all equally human, such respect should be offered in equal measures. The third argument is usually some variation on the 'golden rule'. Health care professionals should provide treatment to others in conformity with the three duties of care because were they to become patients, they would wish to be treated in the same way.

Interpreting the duties of care in practice

The understanding and acceptance of the three duties of care within medicine, along with the professional and philosophical reasons for taking them seriously, are only the beginning of good medical practice. As stated, these duties are little more than moral abstractions. To acquire moral substance, each duty must be interpreted through being applied to particular cases. Sometimes, when the specific circumstances of the case are in obvious conformity or conflict with the duty, then the interpretation is what can be called 'morally determinant'. For example, let us take each duty in turn. Examples of obviously unacceptable professional behaviour would be: (1) mistakenly prescribing a lethal dose of a drug (first duty); (2) not disclosing information about major surgical risks despite being specifically asked (second duty); and (3) refusing to provide urgent treatment to a patient on the grounds of race (third duty). Such examples would inevitably invite professional condemnation and the potential for a legal remedy for the patients concerned.

Unfortunately (or fortunately for medical ethicists!) many clinical cases pose problems of much more moral indeterminacy. Here, there may be disagreement between clinicians, and between clinicians, patients and the public about what course of clinical action is morally and professionally appropriate. This is because the features of such 'hard cases' are on the borderline of inconsistency with one or more of the three duties of care. This may be either because the moral principles subsumed by these duties can conflict with each other; or because there are practical constraints which make compliance with these duties either difficult or impossible. For example, clinicians must have some discretion about the risks that are associated with treatments they prescribe and can disagree about what constitutes an appropriate risk-benefit ratio. Further, the duty to protect life and health can conflict with the duty to respect autonomy. Through either refusing treatment, or being unco-operative in its administration, patients may make it difficult or impossible to protect their life and health successfully. Clinicians can disagree about the most appropriate approach to resolving such conflict. Finally, clinical disagreement is also common about the point at which some patients no longer qualify for life-sustaining treatment and thus about what it means in practice to protect the life and health of patients equally.

Moral indeterminacies of these kinds cannot be resolved by referring back to the duties of care themselves. For the problem is how these duties should be interpreted where there is disagreement about their practical implications. Moral principles do not interpret themselves; they must be interpreted by individuals who, again, may disagree about what constitutes a correct interpretation. When such conflict occurs and appears intractable, the way forward must be to switch the emphasis of discussion away from what might be called 'substantive ethics' towards 'procedural ethics'. This approach to ethics focuses on the most appropriate rules that should govern discussion and debate in order for an optimally rational course of action to be reached in the face of disagreement. For example, discussion should be properly representative, should not be dominated by single vested interests, should ensure that the voices of individual representatives are heard, etc. Here, the goal is to attain the most rational moral solution to the problem at hand, even if this entails moral compromise. In much the same way, clinical indeterminacy about clinical decision-making is most adequately resolved through rigorous and open debate among clinical colleagues.

Professional constraints in interpreting the duties of care

Finally, as has been indicated, agreement on how best to interpret the duties of care in practice does not take place in an organisational or professional vacuum. Without the institutional means to deliver the health care which both substantive and procedural morality dictate to be right, related pronouncements will be of little use to either patients or clinicians. This is because to argue that something should be done entails that it is practically possible to do it ('ought implies can'). Any satisfactory discussion of the ethical principles of medicine must, therefore, examine whatever organisational or professional barriers exist to implementing them in practice.

For example, it may be that tasks considered appropriate to one profession should be shared with or even undertaken by members of another profession to improve the effectiveness and efficiency of health care delivery. Equally, as consultants working in hospital have become more and more specialised, so a vacuum has been created by the absence of those able to fulfil the role of general physician, surgeon or paediatrician. Unfortunately, however, it is difficult for general practitioners to maintain mastery of the broad range of diagnostic information and skills that is necessary, while participating fully in the provision of care and the provision of treatment. It may be, therefore, that for the duties of care to be successfully put into practice throughout the delivery of health care, new divisions of labour concerning shared responsibility will be necessary within a multi-professional team. These may threaten the professional status of those involved and call for new schemes of training and regulation. Current debates about the role of nursing practitioners and PAMs (professions allied to medicine) provide good examples.

Equally, poor educational training and professional regulation can also create other barriers to good clinical practice. Regarding education, the GMC has made it clear that clinicians have a duty to obtain informed consent for treatment and that this will require a competent understanding of related ethico-legal issues as well as competent skills in communicating with patients. Without such understanding and skills, it is simply no good expecting clinicians to practice to a moral standard for which they are ill-equipped. With respect to regulation, therefore, it will be crucial for the regulatory bodies of medicine to become even more rigorous in their insistence that clinical practice always conforms to the duties of care. Poor practice must be revealed and corrected. Yet, without the mechanisms and related resources for improving practice when it is found to be deficient, demands for progress will remain both hollow and hypocritical. It is for this reason that the recent emphasis on clinical governance is to be welcomed. However, more than a welcome will be required to make a difference. It must be accepted within the medical profession that good ethics is just as important for quality in health care as traditional clinical skills.

One thing is clear. Violations of the duties of care which have their roots in poor organisational management or lack of effective training or regulation are no more justifiable than they would be if they were due to the lack of skill or to the carelessness of individual clinicians.

Case analyses

I will now apply my analysis of the duties of care to several cases. In doing so I will assume that the reader has already familiarised themselves with the details of each case (see Chapters 1–5). Sometimes my discussion will address the issues of the cases as they were raised in the accounts given. At other times, it will be necessary to preface specific comments with an outline of other moral arguments which are supplementary to those already discussed.

Ivy Brown

To suffer in silence. When it is practised unreflectively and unethically, medicine can easily let down patients like Ivy Brown. She was passive in the face of insensitive medical authority and too willing to 'suffer in silence', personality traits which may have been deep-seated for a range of cultural and psychological reasons. The first duty of care commands that where medically possible, disability caused by illness is minimised through optimally effective treatment. This did not occur and may have been related to Dr Mason's perceived lack of interest in Mrs Brown. To the degree that this is so, then he was in breach of his third duty of care: not to treat patients differently on the grounds of personal prejudice/preference. This will be the case, irrespective of the clinical appropriateness of his treatment.

Further, Dr Mason also seems not to have been interested in Mrs Brown's autonomy. She appears to have been poorly informed about her condition, her treatment and how to monitor its success. Her lack of understanding clearly fuelled her passivity, illustrating the important links between clinical success and the active and informed involvement of patients as partners in their care. In the face of her own continued suffering, her reticence to seek further help from Dr Mason is a devastating condemnation of his professional ethics. It is also an indication of poor professional practice in reviewing his own actions towards Mrs Brown.

A ray of hope? Dr Wall appears to provide an indication of how things can and should be done in his treatment of Mrs Brown, although it is not clear how much information he managed to communicate about his diagnosis of irritable bowel syndrome. Certainly, he appears to have developed a more constructive relationship with her, especially in light of her willingness to discuss her anxieties concerning her family background and cancer. Yet, he can be criticised for his sweeping assurances that there was no likelihood of her ever developing cancer, given her immediate test results. Being overly optimistic with patients, even anxious ones who may be worried by the truth, can lead to confusion at a later date and possibly an unwillingness to seek medical treatment when it is required.

Discontinuities and technical fixes. Within the general practice involved, there appears to have been no attention paid to continuity of care. This may be because of a lack of clear policy and procedures and/or of rapid staff turnover. Given Mrs Brown's prior history, it is likely that by the time she had seen Dr Stone she would have been most unclear about either what might be wrong with her or what she could legitimately expect from her carers. This would have reinforced her problems concerning active participation in her treatment decisions and may have influenced Dr Stone's unacceptable decision not to give her the option of an informed choice about his prescribed triple treatment. Had she been told of the risk of pseudo membranous colitis, she might have rejected the treatment or not have waited so long to contact Dr Wall after the onset of her much more worrying symptoms. Dr Stone should have more widely consulted with clinical colleagues and, if available, clinical guidelines about the advisability of the triple treatment in someone with Mrs Brown's history and presenting symptoms. General practitioners often find themselves in situations where proper clinical consultation is difficult and organisational steps should be taken to minimise the risks of mistakes that this can bring about.

Hospital knows best? Mrs Brown's hospital treatment seems to have again ignored her right to be consulted about her care. In light of his good relationship with her, Dr Wall might have helped with this but was not contacted as he should have been and was unable to make contact. The organisational interface between primary and secondary care is important for the delivery of continuity of care and it is shown here to have been deficient. Further, it is unclear from the clinical details provided whether or not all of the interventions which were performed were therapeutically necessary (e.g. removal of her colon). Even though Mrs Brown was in an acute condition on admission, it is equally unclear what, if anything, was communicated to her (assuming that she was able to communicate) before her surgery. Without such communication – either in hospital or earlier with Dr Wall – Mrs Brown's final outcome was horrendous. Her general level of poor understanding of her condition and treatment certainly ruined whatever chance she had of ending her life at peace with herself and her family.

Treating the relatives. The response of the clinical team to Mrs Brown's demands was the final insult to her rights and dignity. Returning to the first duty of care, any treatment she received should have been justified with respect to her best interests. Against the background of his apparent clinical judgement about the futility of further care, the consultant should not have bent to the wishes of her family in the way described. The autonomy of family members should be respected in such circumstances in that they should be consulted about patients' best interests and prior wishes. However, they have neither the moral nor the legal right to overrule a properly formulated medical judgement about such interests. The duties to families must not be confused with those owed to patients.

The fact that Mrs Brown was kept alive for 17 days of increasingly pointless but uncomfortable therapeutic interventions cannot be morally or legally justified. It seems clear that it should have been apparent earlier that further active (rather than palliative) intervention was not in her best interest. This is because of the degree to which she was imminently and irreversibly close to death.

One wonders whether or not the consultant's unacceptable behaviour was more a function of his anxiety about being sued than of his desire to be a good doctor.

Conclusion. In the case of Mrs Brown, all three duties of care were repeatedly compromised or ignored altogether. The reasons were both attitudinal and organisational. Attitudinally, her GPs were insufficiently concerned with her understanding of her situation and with their educational as well as therapeutic responsibilities. Organisationally, there was poor communication and follow up between clinicians – both between GPs in the practice and between the practice and the hospital where Mrs Brown met her ghastly end. Individually, many of the doctors involved also demonstrated poor communication skills. Whether or not the former or the latter may have played a causal part in her end is unclear from the details of the case provided.

Father John

A Roman Catholic priest in physical but not spiritual decline. Father John spent his life giving witness to his deep faith as a Christian. Given Church doctrine, he had every reason not to fear death for precisely the same reasons that characterised Basil Hume's emotional approach to his own death. Father John had had a good innings and expected even better to come. In the face of his coronary thrombosis, and with the help of his godson, Father John executed an advance directive that if he got worse he should not be given active treatment. Unfortunately, his consultant failed to make a note of his wishes in his medical record. However, given the presence of his godson and his clinician, along with their presumed willingness to confirm that these were his wishes, Father John's verbal directive had both moral and legal standing. Morally, he autonomously rejected further treatment and according to the second duty of care, this should have been respected. Legally, his treatment constituted a battery had his wishes been properly communicated to the hospital team after his emergency admission.

Admission to coronary care. Despite his verbal advance directive, Father John was successfully resuscitated following his cardiac arrest. In light of the first duty of care, his carers had no professional option, given their lack of information about his general condition and wishes. Dr Marks, his GP, must bear some responsibility for this. As soon as he was back on duty, he should have checked on Father John's progress and provided his carers with further needed details about his condition and background. However, what then transpired was a breach of both the first and second duties of care.

On the one hand, the cardiac team appear to have been more concerned with keeping Father John alive than asking whether or not further life-sustaining treatment was in his best interests. As with Ivy Brown, if patients are physically or mentally suffering and are imminently and irreversibly close to death then further non-palliative treatment cannot be justified. Of course, what 'imminent and irreversible' means will always be a matter of interpretation and, therefore, potentially subject to disagreement. However, in this case there seems little cause for it. On the other hand, the clinical team was breaking the law in ignoring the wishes of Father John, assuming that these were properly communicated as an advance directive by the godson. They may have been unaware that they were doing so due to their poor ethical and legal education, a matter to which schools of medicine are increasingly addressing themselves. This may be behind the confusion (exhibited throughout wider society) about the sanctity of life and the moral and legal circumstances in which life-sustaining treatment can and should be withdrawn. The unwillingness of the team initially to provide Father John with morphine may be further evidence of poor clinical and/or ethical education about palliative care. It may also indicate an over-sensitivity to the possibility of media investigation.

Conclusion. A fine man was denied the death he wanted and deserved through a breakdown in communication between carers and their poor ethical and legal training. The former highlights the need for organisational prompts and checks, which ensure that professionals live up to their responsibilities. Certainly, nothing about Father John's advance directive appears to have been written in the notes. As for poor ethico-legal education, this can be partly corrected through more resources being provided for undergraduate and postgraduate teaching of ethics and law applied to medicine. It can also be corrected by more effective continued education within medicine, along with clearer and more rigorous professional regulation.

Mary Fisher

Mrs Fisher not being helped at home. Mrs Fisher was an independent and self-reliant woman. In light of her history of adaptability to different environments, and success in raising six children, there is every reason to believe that had she been given the opportunity, she could have dealt well with the physical difficulties created by her illnesses. It is equally clear that because of her wish be self-reliant, she may have underestimated the seriousness of her physical condition and not asked questions or made requests for help when she should have. It is against this background that the initial failure of her care team at home should be judged. Her home care should have been more sustained and she should have been encouraged more by her home carer to seek appropriate medical help.

Mrs Fisher in hospital. The willingness of carers to take advantage of Mrs Fisher's desire to be autonomous is clear from her hospital experience. Organisationally, there was little continuity in her care. Even if individual staff had been working hard to respect Mrs Fisher's autonomy through providing her with an appropriate level of information about her condition and treatment – which they were not – then the organisational management of her care would have still been unethical and unacceptable.

Respect for the autonomy of patients should not be simply reactive – waiting for questions that are then answered. It should be both anticipatory and educative – anticipating what kind of information patients need to have optimal control over decisions about their care and then attempting to provide them with it. In doing neither, the staff appear to have taken advantage of Mrs Fisher's own moral concern for them, their problems and her perception of the priority that should be devoted to her care. Organisational prompts should be in place to ensure that this does not occur, irrespective of the immediate attitudes of staff. For example, a checklisted and monitored discharge procedure would have ensured that Mrs Fisher was not stranded and left without care while she waited for transport. Equally, it is important for patients like Mrs Fisher to be encouraged to ask questions and to be reassured that this is appropriate and acceptable in a clinical environment.

Mrs Fisher at home. Here, her problems of isolation continued, in the face of further poor continuity of care and information about her condition and treatment. By this stage in the story of Mrs Fisher's deterioration, one suspects that on top of the organisational and professional problems outlined, she is being discriminated against because of her age. It is important to recognise the possibility of such inequity in attempting to assess organisational effectiveness. In the case of Mrs Fisher, there clearly were organisational problems, especially concerning continuity of care. However, these may well have been dramatically exacerbated by inappropriate and prejudicial professional attitudes.

More on elderly people in our society. The end of Mrs Fisher's story remains gloomy but contains a ray of light. The gloom is due to the fact that both she and her companions at the day hospital would rather be institutionalised in a caring environment than return to domestic accommodation particularly unsuitable for old and vulnerable people. It is here that Mrs Fisher's story moves us beyond the boundaries of medical care *per se* and into the territory of the dire way in which the basic needs of many elderly people are not satisfactorily met in our society. Here, the need for adequate and appropriate housing is the case in point. Doing something about this problem will require a dramatic reallocation of resources and political courage.

Conclusion. Mrs Fisher has been a responsible and hard-working citizen all her life, giving much to others in the process. The fact that the medical treatment she received was such poor repayment for her contribution to society was due to both organisational and attitudinal reasons related to her care. These reasons were amplified by broader prejudices towards elderly people. The resulting injustices – underlined by the insecurity and inappropriateness of her housing in her last years – indicates the degree to which ethics in medicine cannot be divorced from the quality of the moral fabric of society as a whole.

Chris Adams

Some general observations on the value of life. Chris Adams appears to be a good citizen. He is a teacher, a father and partner. He values his life and it is valued by others to whom he discharges his responsibilities effectively. It can be argued that Mr Adams has earned the right to be treated equally with all other humans through the way in which he has lived his life. If we assume that a treatment exists which will enable him to continue to live and to do at least some of the things which he values life for, his need for such a treatment is as great as any need can be. We need physical and mental health because without them we will not be able socially to participate with others in order to achieve whatever life goals we have – in order to flourish as a person. Yet, the most fundamental precondition for physical and mental health is life itself.

The NHS is based on a simple moral creed: equal access to care on the basis of equal need – free at the point of delivery. Adherence to the third duty of care for fairness demands that scarce health care resources be rationed in conformity with this creed. Such rationing can occur provided that it is based on a system of fair waiting (equal access) and that those who do wait are triaged according to the urgency of their condition (morally similar categories of need). The most urgent category of need, again, is for life itself, always providing that the life in question can then be used by the individual to accomplish other life goals to which they and others attach value. It is because of the force of this argument that patients waiting in A&E will not complain about someone in an acute, life-threatening situation being treated before them. Similar arguments apply to the ways in which treatments either are or should be prioritised in the delivery of other clinical specialisations.

The existence of scarce health care resources and of the personal difficulties which this poses for those who are denied care does not in itself take moral priority over the professional imperative to use such resources to save life (again, provided that this life can be directed toward the achievement of goals deemed of value by the person whose life it is). In this sense, life itself is of more moral value than a range of other disabled physical or mental states that are still compatible with some form of self-directed activity. In other words, we would normally rather be alive and physically disabled – at least to a degree – than dead. This is the flaw in arguments which suggest that it might be morally acceptable to allow people to die whom it may be very expensive to save, in order to provide more help to more people with less acute conditions. It is this argument which is implicitly appealed to – though not morally defended – in noting that the provision of further Factor VIIa and a liver transplant for Mr Adams would prevent 100 hip replacements taking place.

Therefore, the description of the dilemma facing the health authority over Mr Adams is misleading. Only the existence of severe scarcity of health care provision is mentioned for the population served by the authority. In fact, as we have seen, an equally important part of the background to the dilemma is the moral foundation of the NHS itself and related moral arguments about fairness, justice and the value of life. To this degree, the advice provided by the lawyers – that Mr Adams should be treated – is sound. The lawyers' advice also reinforced the moral argument that it would be a violation of the third duty of care to prioritise the less urgent needs of many patients over Mr Adams' need for life.

Finally, the case description outlines a severe shortage in the funds allocated to the health authority – an £18–£27 million overspend in one of the most deprived populations in the country. While arguments may go on about the degree to which such an overspend was due to organisational inefficiency, to waste related to ineffective treatment or to simple underfunding from the centre, any or all of these problems will take time to resolve. The difficulties in doing so are substantial. For example, there is little evidence to support the belief that the experiment with the internal market over the last decade led to any substantial savings related to increased efficiency. Conversely, what is clear is that the NHS provides high value for money when compared with other European health care systems and the system in the USA.

Therefore, in considering the problems of Mr Adams, it should not be simply assumed that the size of the cake of NHS expenditure should go unquestioned. Certainly, long lead times for the achievement of greater efficiencies will inevitably mean that individuals requiring expensive treatments for acute conditions in the here and now may carry huge opportunity costs as regards the less expensive treatment of others in less dramatic clinical need. Morally – assuming that the need of the patients is real and that proposed treatment is not futile – the only coherent answer to the dilemma is either the provision of one-off funding from the centre for expensive treatments or a general increase of funding for the NHS overall. Either would reduce the financial shortfall at the heart of Mr Adams' problem.

Did Mr Adams really need transplantation? From the outline of this case, it is not clear how effective a liver transplant would be in treating Mr Adams. As far as his health care team was concerned, there must have been some evidence to suggest that a transplant might be successful, despite his medical condition. It must be assumed (the case summary is not clear on this) that the discussion which then ensued about the provision of transplantation properly analysed the relevant literature for evidence of effectiveness and concluded that his 'slender' chance of success still included a significant possibility that he might survive the surgery. The fact that Mr Adams did survive and 'seemed to make a good recovery initially' confirms the correctness of this appraisal. It was apparently his rejection of his new liver, rather than his haemophilia, that eventually killed him.

Had there been sufficient clinical consensus to maintain convincingly that transplantation could not succeed in anyone in Mr Adam's condition, then it should not have been offered to him. Legally, there is no obligation to offer treatment clinically agreed to be futile. Morally, it is unacceptable to use scarce resources ineffectively just to buy hope. To do so is a violation of the third duty of care in that favouritism is shown toward those with unrealistic hope rather than those in real need. Here, no clear violation of this kind appears to have occurred and the provision of the transplantation for Mr Adams was thus appropriate.

However, having argued for such appropriateness, the moral and clinical indeterminacies of this case should not be underestimated. There can be no doubt that the decision to proceed with transplantation, despite Mr Adams' slender chance of success, will weigh heavily on those patients forced to wait further for their need for appropriate medical care. What is crucial in the face of such indeterminancies is good procedural ethics – that the most rational discussion occurs about the best course of action. If moral compromise is inevitable, it should be the most reasonable one possible in the face of the available evidence. In this case, provisions did seem to be in place for appropriate deliberation. Procedurally, the rules for such deliberation are crucial to ensure that scarce resources are not wasted through ineffectiveness. What rules of this kind should not do, however, is to tamper with the moral foundation of the NHS and to advocate treating patients unequally with morally similar categories of need. For example, such unequal treatment cannot and should not be justified through appeals to the public popularity of some clinical conditions over others.

Conclusion. On the face of it, both the health authority and the clinical team did the best they could for Mr Adams and weighed up the implications of his treatment for other patients. Neither group neglected the opportunity costs for others of treating him. We must presume that his clinicians properly evaluated available clinical evidence about potential effectiveness. The health authority took independent legal advice in its own discussions about the appropriateness of not providing treatment. The moral claim of Mr Adams' acute condition was taken seriously, both by the provision of Factor VIIa and the speedy arrangement for a liver transplant. So even given the uncertainty about the effectiveness of his transplant, Mr Adams' clinicians were justified in proceeding. His life was at risk and there was some evidence that transplantation would work. From Mr Adams' perspective, there was no gamble in this. Without treatment he would certainly have died. Equally, as we have seen, it would have been immoral and unprofessional to allow him to die without the chance that transplantation provided, simply because of its immediate expense or the opportunity costs to others requiring less urgent treatment.

In fact, by the end, Mr Adams' treatment did not cost the envisaged maximum of £1 million a year. Other patients in less need were not as negatively affected as they might have been if Mr Adams had lived. Yet one thing is clear. Only Mr Adams was in a position to place an accurate value on the life gained for him by whatever was spent.

Luke Warm Luke

An aside on the nature of human rights. Rights are claims on others which are believed to be appropriate and, if legal, enforceable. Thus to the degree that rights are believed to exist they then entail duties to act in conformity with them. This will be so irrespective of the preferences of those who might not wish to assume such duties. For example, if we have the right to use our property as we wish or to exercise our freedom of speech then this will be so even if some might prefer otherwise. Yet human rights are not limitless. Our rights cease at the point at which respect for them causes, or risks causing, serious harm to others. If, for example, we wish to use our private property or to express our freedom of speech in ways that will or may be harmful in this sense, these rights will be correspondingly curtailed. For the same reason, within medicine, clear limits are placed on the right of patients to confidentiality. Both morally and legally, if respect for this right places others in danger then the confidence can be broken to the degree that protection of the public can be assured. For example, in the famous legal case *W v. Egdell* (1993), a psychiatrist who broke the confidentiality of his patient was exonerated on precisely these grounds.

Further, if rights are conceived as legitimate claims on others, respect for rights will be proportional to the capacity of the rights bearer to make appropriate claims. For example, we have seen that in medicine, the second duty of care dictates that patients have the right to have their autonomy respected by their clinicians. Yet, the degree to which this holds for children will depend on the extent of their autonomy – their degree of maturity to provide consent to treatment that can be said to be truly informed. To the degree that they cannot do so, then they can be said to be in the control of their immaturity rather than in control of their lives. For this reason, protection is the foremost moral duty of a clinician confronted with such a child patient. Here, the first duty of care takes precedence over the second duty to respect autonomy, whereas with competent adults (e.g. who have the right to refuse life-sustaining treatment) it is the other way around. Precisely the same argument applies to patients with serious psychiatric illness – who are controlled by their illness rather than in control.

Finally, since rights are proportional to the possession of the ability to make related claims on others, when such abilities are diminished, duties that are associated with rights are not altogether abolished. Rather, those with relevant duties are morally (and perhaps legally) required to respect the *degree* of ability of the right holder to make appropriate claims. For example, just because the autonomy of a child has been reduced as a result of their age does not entail that they have no autonomy. Depending on a range of factors associated with maturity, they will have some ability to make decisions for themselves but not necessarily enough ability to command the respect of full maturity. In such circumstances, it will be the moral and legal duty of their clinician to respect as much autonomy as they do possess – through consulting them about their views and trying to implement their wishes in ways which are consistent with their overall clinical protection.

The same arguments hold for psychiatric treatment and, specifically, for Luke Warm Luke. Adult psychiatric patients who are competent to make decisions about their mental health have, and should have, all of the rights associated with the second duty of care. For example, their right to consent to or refuse all types of medical treatment should be respected, including psychiatric treatment. For a small minority, their illness will be so extreme that the illness is in control of some of the patient's actions. When this is so and patients become a danger to themselves or to others then, as in the case of children, the moral emphasis of the duties of care becomes focused on protection rather than on respect for their autonomy. Therefore if they refuse a prescribed treatment which will offer such protection then it becomes morally and legally justifiable to force such treatment on them. Indeed, given the first duty of care, the use of such compulsion becomes a professional duty.

Yet, as with impact of immaturity on children, the existence of the duty to administer treatment/protection compulsorily to psychiatric patients can be justified only to the degree that the patient lacks the competence to refuse it. If they possess such competence then their autonomy must be respected even if they pose a risk to themselves or others. For example, suicidal acts are tolerated in our society, as is the freedom of those who are known to be potential criminals but who cannot be shown to have committed criminal acts. Equally, just because a psychiatric patient has been deemed to be incompetent to make informed choices about their mental health does not entail that they are similarly incompetent to consent to or refuse other forms of treatment for physical disorders. Unless there is good reason to believe that such incompetence exists, patients who have been sectioned under the Mental Health Act must still give their consent to such treatment.

In short, it is the duty of psychiatrists and the psychiatric team to protect life and health within the context of respect for as much autonomy as is present in patients. Because of the well-known indeterminacies associated with the diagnosis of psychiatric illness, this can be fraught with difficulty. Due the stigma associated with such illness, misdiagnosis also poses serious dangers for patients. The care and caution that is rightly used in the administration of the Mental Health Act should be seen in this light. However, there can be no doubt that whatever the degree of such indeterminacy, the duty to protect life supersedes the desire for diagnostic and therapeutic certainty. The evaluation of what happened to Luke Warm Luke must be seen in this light.

Why such disastrous continuity of care for Luke Warm Luke?

There can be no doubt that Luke Warm Luke's care was characterised by both indecision and discontinuity. On the one hand, he was clearly suffering from a serious and treatable psychiatric illness that put others at great risk. On the other hand, from the very beginning there was unwillingness to institutionalise him for sustained treatment even though he consistently refused to take his medication. Time and again, he had to commit violence to receive the protection that he and his victims deserved. Yet he received it only in different venues where long-term relationships of trust would have been difficult to develop. To this degree, there was a willingness on the part of successive psychiatric teams to place his autonomy before the public interest, even though it must have been understood that without proper medication his competence to make informed choices was dangerously compromised. The most devastating decision in this regard was that of the consultant who agreed to the discontinuation of his medication while he was living in the community. With hindsight, the consequences of doing so were probably inevitable.

This sequence of questionable clinical management may have been due to ineffective communication between the various clinicians who were responsible for Luke Warm Luke's care. This can be a problem between different clinical teams within one institution. In his case, Luke being passed between different teams within different institutions compounded this problem. Without accurate information about his history, especially the details of his history of violence, it is easy to understand the temptation of his clinicians to underestimate the danger he posed for others. After all, their clinical task was to help him enhance his autonomy, something that seems inconsistent with institutionalising him and forcing him to comply with treatment. For this reason, along with the serious threat to the public of a mistaken discharge into the community, it is important to develop discharge procedures that are not in the control of only one consultant. As we have seen, it is only through an emphasis on such procedural ethics that the moral indeterminacies associated with the Mental Health Act can be minimised. As Luke Warm Luke illustrates, such minimisation is imperative.

Three ways to try to ensure that the story of Luke Warm Luke does not repeat itself. First, Luke Warm Luke represents a failure of the national policy to maximise effective psychiatric treatment in the community. It is now widely accepted that for some patients – irrespective of the danger they pose to others – this policy is unacceptable as it now works. Their successful treatment sometimes requires a secure long-term institutional environment where compliance to treatment can be properly monitored and where risks of harm can be minimised. To the degree that the closure of so many mental hospitals is the reason for not providing such sustained care, new hospitals should be built and the national policy reversed. It is striking in Luke's story that the only times he successfully responded to treatment were when he was in a secure institutional environment. Whenever he was in the community, he was unable to comply with treatment. On the face of it, therefore, Luke Warm Luke, the woman he killed and the people he attacked were all let down by a policy that did not provide him with the therapeutic environment that he so desperately needed.

Second, it is possible that if a way could have been found to force Luke Warm Luke to comply with treatment, he might well have been successfully treated in the community. Unfortunately, the Mental Health Act currently makes this impossible, as there are no provisions for compulsory medication after discharge from hospital. Were things otherwise, Luke would have had to choose which was more important to him: his physical freedom or his freedom to refuse treatment. It is understandable why some seriously ill psychiatric patients do not want to take their medications. They do not like the side effects or the perceived diminution of autonomy that they experience as a result of them. Yet, if refusal to comply with treatment leads to reduced autonomy – not to mention danger – then the moral imperative to respect autonomy will also be diminished. It is this fact that provides an acceptable moral justification for arguing that the Mental Health Act be changed to make enforced medication possible for some patients whom it may be advisable to discharge from hospital. However, given the threat to civil liberties that such a move entails, it is also the case that more procedurally secure methods of associated diagnosis need to be developed. For example, as was the case with Ivy Brown, it would be inadvisable for individual consultants to have powers of such compulsion. Issues concerning the protection of patients' confidentiality in such a setting would also have to be addressed.

Third, health care professionals should be better educated, both on law and on their moral responsibilities towards others. On several occasions, decisions were made not to institutionalise Luke Warm Luke that may have been informed by an incorrect reading of the Mental Health Act. In fact, it is a highly flexible instrument for such purposes (some critics say too flexible). Equally, inappropriately allowing Luke his freedom may also have been caused by a lack of due moral concern for the protection of the public. The fact that the duty of clinical care does not legally extend beyond the individual patient does not entail that this should be the case morally. Weighing up the moral demands of one against those of the other is not easy. It requires training and education in ethics and law applied to medicine, much more than is currently on offer in most medical schools.

Conclusion. Luke Warm Luke was let down by his individual clinicians who appeared unsure about both his diagnosis and his proper management. While there is more clinical indeterminacy within psychiatry than in other branches of medicine, this cannot explain the variability of diagnosis and lack of coherent continuity of care. Generally, his carers were too unwilling to treat him in an institutional environment for a long period, a problem made more severe by the current shortage of appropriate mental hospitals. Another reason for their ineffective care may have been moral confusion about the priority that should be placed on Luke's autonomy in the face of the threat that he posed to the public. A much more aggressive policy of protection of the public is perfectly compatible with consistent moral analysis and with the Mental Health Act. However, what is problematic about the Act is the barrier it poses for the administration of compulsory medication within the community.

Chapter 8

Public health challenges for the new millennium

Deirdre Cunningham

Introduction

This chapter identifies public health issues from the five case histories. It discusses the themes, both in relation to the case histories and generally, with a view to informing the discussions about the values that should underpin the work of the NHS and health care in the new millennium.

The underlying impression gained from the histories is of a health care system too rigid and inflexible to take into consideration individual patients' wishes. It is a system that may have developed its ways of operating or rules based on what was thought to be in the best interests of patients originally, but which is currently serving its own purposes as much as those of the patient; a system short of resources in which efforts to contain the use of those resources are resulting in further inefficiency, lack of humanity and inequity. These cases 'feel' real and scenarios like these could be happening every day throughout the country. The main issue is: how we can treat patients and the public more humanely, in a culture of finite resources, and what are the public health consequences of not doing so? Specific questions raised by the cases are discussed below.

Who is the service for?

What is it that public sector services, and particularly the NHS, are trying to achieve, and for whom? The traditional public health dilemma is whether it is aimed at the needs of populations or of individuals (see 'Where does the boundary lie between the rights of populations and individuals?' below). But if these five cases are typical, it is difficult to relate what happens to patients to their wishes at all. The services seem to be aiming at clinical end points unrelated to patients' wishes – or even in some cases their best interests – and when services do take individual patients' wishes into consideration (Chris Adams and Luke Warm Luke), the population as a whole is potentially or actually harmed. Ivy's, Father John's and Mary Fisher's wishes were either ignored or not considered.

For example, Ivy received poor treatment from a locum doctor who ignored established guidelines and her needs and this eventually resulted in her receiving inappropriate high-tech care. Father John's wishes were ignored, even though as a Catholic priest he might be assumed to have been preparing himself for death. As a consultant at an ethics seminar on withdrawing treatment said in relation to an A&E department, 'you abandon autonomy as you walk into this hospital'. That seems to have been the case for Father John and Ivy.

Mary Fisher's needs could have been met in a simple low-tech way, probably better by the local authority and local networks. But no one asked her what her needs were. In fact, her care seemed to lack any clear sense of purpose. Her autonomy was also ignored and her treatment verged on the paternalistic.

So, if Ivy, Father John and Mary Fisher were treated without consideration with regard to their wishes, and they were all old, what about Chris and Luke Warm Luke? Chris's views and autonomy were respected and his treatment was funded even though by doing so treatment for many other individuals (possibly old) was sacrificed. And Luke's wish not to experience the side effects of drugs was also respected, but at what cost to society? The public's rights in this case were taken less seriously than that of the individual.

If these cases are typical – and they may be – health care appears not to be concerned with the clinical end points, nor with the cultural or quality requirements of individuals (particularly of older individuals), but rather to be concerned with those dictated by the service or the setting. If patients are unfortunate enough to arrive in an acute hospital setting in the final stages of their lives, possibly through a chapter of accidents, they appear to get the service which that setting is designed to deliver, regardless of their needs. This could be obviated by ensuring that their care plan is co-ordinated by a team, or by a holistic physician such as a geriatrician.

The decision when to stop treatment for these cases is also an important one. The result, in public health terms, is possibly a whole care group in the population – elderly people – who have reason to fear health care and those who deliver it, and who have very little expectation of what it can do (e.g. Mary Fisher). Health care could prevent further deterioration for many of our elderly population, minimise disability and, where human warmth is required, could encourage its provision. This would do a great deal to ensure that people had healthier, more confident and less disabled later years, and would also free up an enormous resource in terms of intensive therapy unit (ITU) and acute hospital facilities which are currently denied to others who may need them more. Currently, at least 40 per cent of NHS resources are spent on people of 65 and over.[1] As the proportion of the population who are elderly is predicted to rise, this situation is likely to be exacerbated in the future. Age is a major determinant of NHS spending, which makes it all the more important to use such resources wisely, to maximum effect.

For the population in general, the individual's wishes seemed to have been listened to more than the views of the public whose interests may have been put at risk by this. The public opportunity cost of funding hugely expensive cases with no additional money or of valuing the liberty and freedom of potentially harmful individuals should be widely debated, though no easy solution will emerge.

Why can't there be better communication?

If services are designed to meet the needs of either patients or the population, good communication between different parts of the service, and between the service and patients, carers and relatives is essential to ensure not only an efficient service, but also an effective and appropriate one. Yet failure of communication is apparent in at least four of the five cases.

For instance, Ivy's risk was not adequately communicated to her, and there was no communication between her GP and the locum. In her final days, there was inadequate communication between and within the clinical teams, and between the teams and Ivy's relatives. In Father John's case, there was a failure of communication with the deputising doctor and also no evidence that staff had looked for his notes, or made efforts to know of his or his relatives' wishes.

Mary Fisher had no idea why she was receiving the care she did receive, and communication breakdown was the reason for her being 'lost to transport'. Ivy did not even bother to ask what was happening to her, her expectations were so low. And Luke Warm Luke's story may have included confidentiality as a reason for not sharing some information, but throughout, his care lacked communication and planning between his carers.

A number of public health issues could be highlighted here:

- a failure adequately to communicate risk to individuals about to undergo a treatment for which the rationale is based on population benefit: this may not only harm the individual, but ultimately the population programme, e.g. immunisation. The public may become increasingly suspicious of such programmes and refuse to participate. An example is the suspicion surrounding the mumps, measles and rubella programme (MMR) following adverse publicity which, once published, is difficult to counter, and yet an outbreak of measles is predicted for the year 2001[2]

- a failure of different professionals caring for individuals to communicate their care plan or wishes, resulting in inappropriate care aimed at the wrong end points in the wrong setting. This can be a particular issue where locums are involved. The result is to provoke fear and mistrust of professionals by the public, and a waste of scarce NHS resources

- a failure of different clinicians to communicate between themselves and with relatives about stopping and starting treatment which is in the patients' (and ultimately the population's) best interests, results in inappropriate decisions for patients and the public

- a failure of communication between those caring for individuals who are potentially dangerous puts not only the individual but also the wider public at risk.

It may be thought that the NHS's latest information strategy, *Information for Health,* will solve the problems. But it will only do so if professionals feel that the information is important and *use* it.

Where does the boundary lie between the rights of populations and individuals?

The NHS/health care system is essentially a population programme designed to provide comprehensive treatment to the population of England while being sensitive to individuals. The Government's commitment is that 'if you are ill or injured there will be a National Health Service there to help; and access to it will be based on need and need alone'.[3] However, it is essential to agree what the responsibilities of the service are to individuals and what they are to the public, and to agree to accept the risks involved in 'serving two masters'. These case studies suggest that the boundaries have not been defined clearly enough.

For example, if the locum doctor had been conforming to accepted clinical guidelines and offering Ivy treatment designed largely to eradicate Helicobacter pylori in population terms, he was nevertheless incurring a risk for Ivy. She should have had that risk communicated to her *and* he should have undertaken appropriately sensitive and specific tests for that risk.

Chris's treatment was not only risky for him; it could also put the health care of others at risk. A liver transplant is risky particularly for a patient with a bleeding tendency, but by giving him such treatment, a substantial proportion of the local NHS budget was tied up in one patient, thus potentially denying others treatment. And Luke Warm Luke's individual rights were respected to a certain extent more than those of the general public.

The public health issues are that all population programmes pose some risk to the individuals concerned, and that they must realise this and agree to it. In some cases, it is important for public health that individuals take that risk for the greater good (e.g. immunisation) but in the case of Helicobacter that is not the case. The second point is that for a patient who has exhausted all other forms of treatment and therefore is at risk of dying, any expensive new treatment cannot be properly evaluated for use for that patient's particular circumstances and is therefore provided at risk. It may well not work, as in Chris's case. However, funding such a treatment from a finite local budget at the expense of the general population is a risk in itself and makes the public suffer. The question arises as to whether such decisions should be taken and funded centrally, which would avoid local opportunity costs and make for fairer, more equitable decisions.

The third point is whether we have got right the boundary between individual psychiatric patients' rights and the rights of the public to protection (over 30 homicide enquiries are currently underway in London). There is also an issue as to whether the resource-conserving decision not to fund newer anti-psychotics, possibly with fewer side effects, is a false economy if the side effects of traditional anti-psychotic medication result in patients not accepting treatment. The homicide enquiries alone must be at least ten times the cost of the drugs.

Why can't we admit we need to ration resources and do it properly and fairly?

In all cases, decisions about fair shares and rationing were involved but largely in a covert fashion. Father John used intensive facilities that could have been devoted to others who needed them more and tied up teams of staff who could have been better deployed. Not only was his treatment inhumane and culturally unacceptable for him, but others may have been denied treatment. Mary Fisher's not eating went unnoticed, possibly due to social services' resource cuts affecting meals on wheels – another false economy perhaps – and her fragmented and unsatisfactory treatment could have been due in part to nursing resource shortages. Her early discharge may have been due to shorter lengths of stay, possibly resulting from the pressure on acute services to stay within budget and increase activity, or to the Private Finance Initiative (PFI). There is evidence that the public-private partnership in hospital capital developments is resulting in shorter lengths of stay not necessarily dictated by patient need.

Luke Warm Luke was denied drugs with potentially fewer side effects, possibly because of resource constraints, while Chris was not denied treatment, but his (unsuccessful) treatment cost approximately the same as 100 hip replacements.

Chronic resource shortage could be leading to covert rationing which discriminates against vulnerable or less favoured groups, such as elderly people (Mary Fisher, Father John), racial groups (Luke) or those suffering from mental illness (Luke); whereas Chris was thought worthy of treatment possibly because he was relatively young and had children and a job (a productive member of society). If covert forms of rationing are applied, discrimination against groups (e.g. ageism) and variation will occur. The decision-making process should be transparent and explicit. If the NHS cannot 'cover' all forms of care, or bear all risks, it should say so. And if one care group such as elderly people accounts for nearly half of the NHS spend, it is crucial that these resources are well spent.

Chris's high-cost case could have been funded nationally without allowing residents of one area to suffer, or it could have been made explicit that the NHS cannot be expected to bear such a cost for one individual. This, however, may be unacceptable politically. Even if it were decided to override the rights of an individual in the interests of the population at large, the political repercussions of such a decision may be too serious to even consider it. Whether to start treatment at all was an issue for Chris. Whether and when to stop treatment was equally an issue for Ivy and Father John.

Should evidence of effectiveness and appropriateness be required for such decisions? Decisions 'on the edge' rely less on evidence and more on 'compassion',[4] because both the clinical condition and the treatment may be new and relatively uncharted. Nor has the NHS defined the 'cost of a life'. Any hope may seem justified when all else is exhausted, and the public and the media appear to expect the NHS to come to the rescue. Possibly the most humane solution is to rely on compassion as the criterion, because we can see from Father John and Ivy's cases that continuing expensive treatment can be less than compassionate – the opposite in fact.

Economies in Luke's treatment and the availability of staff to treat him may have been false economies, but are understandable, given sectoral budget constraints. However, economies due to funding arrangements may be made in one sector, which have implications for other sectors. People with mental health problems may not be perceived as deserving extra resources as much as patients like Chris, and in Luke's case, there may be underlying race issues, as a high proportion of people with schizophrenia (particularly in major cities) may be of Afro-Caribbean origin.

Why can't we achieve continuity of care and care in the right setting?

Ivy, Father John and Mary Fisher received care in the wrong setting. What Mary needed was human warmth and company: what she got was neglect rather than treatment, and then a day hospital because there was nowhere else to go. Nursing continuity would have avoided her being 'lost to transport', but not getting into hospital in the first place would have been preferable.

Public health issues include how we design services to meet patients' needs, while still meeting requirements for sub-specialisation, clinical governance, training etc., and how we have the right quantity of resources available to meet individual and public needs.

Why can't quality be better?

Poor primary care was a feature of the care of Ivy, Father John, Mary Fisher (where *was* primary care?), and poor locum arrangements was an important factor in two cases. Yet, quality cannot be measured simply in terms of whether effective treatment is delivered. If quality is seen as providing the right treatment to meet the patient's needs, all but Chris suffered poor quality care. Poor quality of care for elderly people with many different health problems was demonstrated by the treatment of Father John and Mary Fisher. And a similar lack of planning or care management was seen in Luke's case.

The model of care received by elderly or vulnerable people is crucial for decision-making and a matter of concern to both individuals and the public. Lack of planning for our elderly population and lack of involvement of generalists with special expertise in dealing with elderly people (geriatricians) will result in a lack of balance of prevention, health promotion and rehabilitation as well as treatment. This is likely to lead to the complete opposite of what the Government is trying to achieve in *Saving Lives*,[5] namely a healthier, less disabled, happier and longer-living population.

Luke's treatment seemed more like punishment than treatment. If quality cannot be improved for the mentally ill then the number of suicides and homicides will continue to increase. However, there is evidence that 'divided societies' produce more mental illness, drug and alcohol misuse, suicide and homicides.[6] So, if the Government's new programme really works to reduce the inequalities gap, it may also result in reducing the (mental) health gap.[7]

Conclusion

These five case histories strike at the heart of what health care is all about and for whom. The new millennium might offer us the opportunity to rethink some of the fundamental principles and design a health care system which makes the best use of what are always likely to be finite resources, and which is clearly aimed at the population and people it is serving. Nevertheless, it must be acknowledged that there will always be dilemmas in balancing the needs of the population as a whole and of individuals, and these must be the subject of continuing debate.

References

1. NHS Executive. *1999/2000 Health Authority Revenue Allocations Exposition Book.* Leeds: NHS Executive, 1998.

2. Begg N, Ramsay M and Bozoky Z. Media dents confidence in MMR vaccine. *BMJ* 1998; 316: 561.

3. Department of Health. *The New NHS: modern, dependable.* London: HMSO, 1997.

4. Elster J. The ethics of medical choice. In: Elster J and Herpin N, editors. *The ethics of medical choice; Social change in Western Europe.* London: Pinter, 1994: 1–22.

5. Department of Health. *Saving Lives: Our Healthier Nation.* London: HMSO, 1999.

6. Wilkinson RG. National mortality rates: the impact of inequality? *Am. J. Public Health* 1992; 82(8): 1082–84.

7. Department of Health. *Saving Lives: Our Healthier Nation*. London: HMSO, 1999.

Chapter 9

Challenges for primary care

Alison P Hill

The nature of primary medical care

Most people in the UK obtain all their NHS health care through their general practitioner. The GP is usually the first port of call except when people present their problems in A&E departments. New ways for people to obtain primary care are being offered through projects like NHS Direct and walk-in centres, but these are not, at present, delivering *medical care*, nor are they offering the *comprehensiveness* and *continuity* which form crucial planks of the philosophy and policy of general practice. Most people remain registered with their GP for many years and in small practices doctor and patient get to know each other well. GPs are still, with a few exceptions, providing comprehensive health care as an independent contractor to the health service, employing the staff to help them organise and provide that care, and connecting with other providers to refer their patients for treatment and care they cannot personally provide. Possessive pronouns are used, denoting an ongoing relationship. Primary medical care is different from care provided in other parts of the NHS because of the nature of the therapeutic relationship, its length, its breadth and its intimacy. GPs and their teams work in the community; patients are cared for close to or at home. GP surgeries are often designed to be homely and welcoming. GPs take great care to provide medical care in terms that patients can understand.

The broad scope and the indeterminacy of general medical practice, and the blurred boundaries between the roles of all professionals working in the community setting make it difficult to define primary care precisely. It is interesting that two of the most succinct definitions come from North America, where primary care is less universal, less comprehensive and less personal.*† In the UK, general practice is a clinical specialty in its own right with a 20-year history of well organised and validated professional training, and an increasingly convincing research base. But the specialty grew slowly from a realisation that the practice of medicine in the community was technically as well as socially different from practice in hospital, where most of doctors (and nurses) are trained. Traditional medical practice, orientated towards diagnosis and treatment and based on biological science, did not prepare clinicians for the inchoate and ill-defined health problems they faced in general practice.[1] Disease presents earlier and diagnostic examination or investigation often do not detect it. Most common conditions that present do not require hospital-based diagnosis and treatment. In fact, they may defy such definition, as most illness seen in general practice does not fit textbook definitions of disease. One of the key skills in successful general practice is to know when to refer for further investigation and treatment, and more importantly for most people, when to wait watchfully.

The maturing discipline came to realise that it is more helpful to see a patient's illness in the context of that person's lifestyle, family and community.[2] Problem solving and illness management need to be tailored to the individual. The knowledge accrued by people who live and work in the community with a population of patients they understand, made up of individuals they know, is a powerful aid to effective and economic health care.

---

*'Primary care is first contact, continuous, comprehensive and co-ordinated care provided to individuals and to populations undifferentiated by age, gender, disease or organ system.' Starfield B. Is primary care essential? *Lancet* 1994; 344: 1129–33.

†'Primary care (is) the provision of integrated accessible health care services by clinicians who are accountable for addressing a large majority of personal health care needs, developing a sustained partnership with patients and practising in the context of family and community.' Donaldson MS and Vanselow NA. *J. Fam. Pract.* 1996; 42: 113–16.

Perhaps because primary medical care is a largely home-based and low-tech form of medical practice, or perhaps because of the intimately personal nature of the therapeutic relationship, there has been much emphasis on the consultation itself as the main focus of care, and much effort has been put into developing the consultation or communication skills of primary care clinicians.

Professor Ian McWhinney is widely recognised as an international academic lead for 'family medicine' (recognised as general practice in the UK). He has articulated nine principles that govern the actions of GPs, to which most aspire. His list encapsulates the world view of this professional group and serves as a useful benchmark in thinking about the scope of general practice and the future direction of primary care development.[3]

His principles demonstrate more than a generalist's approach of physicians practising in the community:

- practice is committed to a *person* rather than to a body of knowledge, a part of the body or a technique

- practitioner seeks to understand the *context* of illness

- seeks every opportunity for *prevention* of illness and the promotion of health

- sees the practice as a *population* at risk

- acts as part of a community wide *support network*

- works (and lives) in the same community as patients – '*shared ecology*'

- sees patients in their own *home*

- understands the importance of the *subjective* (phenomenological) aspects of medicine

- manages *resources*.

None of these is unique to primary care physicians, but it is the combination of them that defines the goal and tasks of general practice.

The politician's favourite

In the NHS, patients cannot access more expensive, technical care without the agreement and active intervention by their general practitioner. GPs, as the contractors for the cottage industry of primary medical care, have shown themselves to be flexible, innovative and economically minded. For these reasons they are seen as powerful players in controlling cost and demanding efficient and responsive services. It is this perception among politicians that has placed primary care at the centre of NHS development policy and new patterns of commissioning secondary care.[4,5] As Starfield notes in her international comparison, even without the incentives of the British system where GPs live off the profits of their service provision, primary care is less labour intensive, uses less capital (for premises and equipment) and is less hierarchical in its organisation than specialist medicine. It is therefore inherently more adaptable and capable of responding to changing societal needs.[6]

However, if a professional group is practising according to custom and practice determined by the profession itself, what happens when technical advances or societal changes outstrip what the profession offers, or make its special focus redundant?

A historical review of the medical profession[7] shows that professional custom and practice, and the professions' internal organisational arrangements, do change over time. If the profession fails to meet the needs or expectations of society, then society will find some other way of meeting that need, perhaps turning to a group outside the profession. This means that professions evolve in response to social pressures, sometimes in ways that conflict with the expressed intentions of their members.[8]

Primary medical care in the UK is under pressure to change: its mode of delivery, its focus, its division of labour, its accessibility and organisation, its role in the health service from provider and co-ordinator to commissioner. Should it resist? Can it usefully do so? The case histories demonstrate the difficulty GPs and their teams have in living up to the modes of practice and the responsibilities which, with the state's blessing, they have set themselves.

Evidence-based medicine and everyday practice

Ivy Brown's story demonstrates how different attitudes to practice by doctors with different priorities, knowledge and experience, can affect life for patients. It seems that after a few consultations with Dr Mason an agreement (probably tacit) had been struck, that nothing special should be done about her symptoms. Dr Mason may not have had effective symptomatic treatment available to him. Or it may have been that both he and Ivy accepted the diagnosis and advice in order to avoid conflict arising from repeated dispiriting and ineffective consultations where they simply did not arrive at a shared understanding of the cause and remedy of Ivy's distress.[9]

One of the main tasks of primary care is to understand and to tolerate long-term suffering, because the effective management of primary care problems may not be within the power of conventional medical treatment. However, Dr Mason seems to have made no effort to support Ivy in coming to terms with her symptoms.

Dr Wall joins the practice as an enthusiastic doctor with up-to-date knowledge, keen to base his practice on evidence. He knows a bit about the illness from reading research but has not met many sufferers yet. He decides on a physical examination and investigations based on what he knows from research, medical teaching and what conditions commonly occur. The power of these tests to support or refute the diagnoses that occur to him is questionable. There are concerns that negative results in screening programmes may influence people with symptoms to delay seeking medical attention.

Although the tests which Dr Wall chose were innocuous (unlike some which might have been ordered by a hospital specialist), they may also have caused harm. Had they proved positive they would not have allowed a specific diagnosis to be made (they had a low specificity as diagnostic tools). They might have been false (unreliable), causing Ivy morbid anxiety, and led to more invasive and potentially harmful investigations in order to clarify the situation.

The rest of the story demonstrates the difficulty of maintaining continuity of care and of information. Once Ivy was admitted to hospital it might have helped if Dr Wall had known what was happening and could have visited her to mediate with the hospital staff, or to act as an interpreter for Ivy, a familiar, trusted and knowledgeable person in an alienating environment. GPs have a workload that precludes this kind of activity. Primary and secondary care are so separate that it is difficult for staff to act effectively across the interface.

Discontinuity and communication

The case of Father John also demonstrated problems with communication between doctors in primary care with different priorities and knowledge of the patient, and across the primary-secondary care boundary. Had Dr Marks been on call when John had his second heart attack, would he have sent him to hospital, or provided support and comfort sufficient to allow him to remain in the care of the Sisters at home? If he had decided that admission was the better option, would he have been able to influence the way John was treated in the ITU? It is often difficult for GPs to persuade hospital staff to desist from active treatment and to provide palliative care. Was there some way in which the advance directive could have been notified to the out-of-hours service, or could have been made directly available through the nursing home?

Mary's story also demonstrates problems with communication: between doctor and patient, between staff, and between agencies. No one seemed to be empowering Mary to speak for herself or to want to act as her advocate. The district nurse and doctor clearly had not sat down to work out a proactive strategy for helping Mary recover, and did not understand each others' point of view or contribution to Mary's care.

It was the absence of quite small things like transport home and a lack of attentiveness that caused much of her problems. No one took the trouble to make sure she understood what was being done for her, why and what she might expect. No one seems to have been able to co-ordinate the social and medical aspects of her rehabilitation.

Questions for the future

There are many pressures on primary care: the shortage of doctors and nurses trained to work in primary care; the willingness of the public to access highly technical and specific treatment; perhaps a loss of confidence in the generalist, empirical and expectant approach. Will there be a place for medicine outside hospital? The increasing demand for and access to reliable but impersonal sources of information and medical advice may undermine the role of the primary care practitioner as personal adviser.

There are technological advances that may make it easier for the diagnosis and treatment functions of secondary care to reach out into the community. Is primary care becoming redundant?

Currently patients express a wish for personal care, and, especially when they are sick, welcome the humane and hermeneutic aspects of primary care. Even if a consumerist, quick-fix-for-the-trivial approach suits the middle class minority there still remains a need for a comprehensive, supportive continuous service of care and integrated advice for the vulnerable, the socially excluded and the chronically sick. There is a great deal of difference between the comprehensiveness and inclusiveness that characterise primary health care and the protocol-driven and impersonal nature of the online curiosity service of NHS Direct. So if for economic and humanitarian reasons there is still a case for the existence of a primary care service, there is a need to ensure the continued relevance and viability of primary care. Six questions present themselves from these case studies:

What is the modern task of primary health care?

This will depend on what patients want, what can and should be provided close to home. It is not a matter of filling in the gaps left by the hospital care service, because most people never go near a hospital and trends are towards referring treatment and care back to primary care. However, many doctors and nurses in primary care are growing uneasy at the increased complexity of cases and treatments they are being asked to manage in the patient's home.

With increasing emphasis on patient choice in clinical decisions primary practitioners will, because of their familiarity and the extent to which they are trusted, have a greater role of helping patients understand the options open to them and facilitating their decision-making.

What skills and competencies will be needed?

This will depend on the task. There is no doubt that new skills are called for that will help to facilitate shared decision-making. General practice has long concentrated on high quality communication skills. But research demonstrates that although skills of persuasion may be high, those of listening need more emphasis. If primary care practitioners are to facilitate the patients' role in making decisions about treatment, skills in the management and transfer of information, and in the discussion of risk will be required.[10]

The current concern to promote evidence-based medicine is heightened in primary care because the unique complexity of each patient is particularly prominent, the nature of illness is less specific and recognisable, and factual evidence on effective treatment is derived from carefully controlled studies on highly selected populations. The knowledge base derived from such studies is largely irrelevant to primary care. So in addition to the now traditional primary care priority skills of communication and contextual practice, there needs to be the skill to practice medicine which integrates biological with psychosocial. The development of this skill demands a new knowledge base, which provides the answers to diagnostic, therapeutic and prognostic matters important in primary care.[11]

Who should deliver it?

There has been a three-fold increase in the numbers of nurses working in the community in the past decade, with a wide range of skills and expertise. The specialist nurses and nurse practitioners show different but increasing ability and willingness to work autonomously. As they develop their skills, GPs move to other tasks, and may lose some of their practical skills through disuse, for example in the management of diabetes. The division of labour is based on historical precedent, but may bear very little relevance to the needs of patients, and to what is practical or possible given the reduction in the availability of doctors or the type of training and experience they bring. It also may be economically more sound to further increase the number of nurses and reduce the number of doctors, moving more of the traditional tasks of medicine to nurses.[12]

What technological support will be required?

If primary care is to provide better co-ordination of care and support, the opportunities offered by technological advances will help. Dr Wall might have been able to have a clearer idea of Ivy Brown's risk of developing bowel cancer if he had known her genome. If Dr Stone had Ivy's genetic profile available, on a smart card, or in her electronic record, he might have known the risks of her not tolerating triple therapy and taken some other course of action. If he had had direct access to more discriminatory diagnostic tests he may not have felt obliged to treat her with potentially toxic therapy on a 'try it and see' basis of empirical diagnosis. If Dr Wall or Dr Marks had had electronic real time access to their patients' records as they suffered in hospital, they might have been better able to intervene on their behalf.

What organisational arrangements might be most effective?

The small practice where patients feel that the staff know them well remains popular. Will the need to control cost and standardise the quality of primary care provision lead to the demise of the cottage industry? Will NHS Direct and walk-in centres be a useful addition to general practice-based care, or will it undermine the integrated model of care? Will larger primary care trusts carry the incentives for the economic provision of care? Will they have the flexibility to respond to the need of local diversity in the population and to the needs of individuals?

How important is continuity of care?

Disjointed service provision caused trouble for most of the people in our case studies. So much reliance was placed on the knowledge carried by individuals. Yet it is the soft knowledge and recognition of longstanding and personal relationships that can contribute to the quality of care, the patient's satisfaction with it, and the professional's motivation to continue. It is a key component of the trust that seems to be crucial for successful therapeutic relationships, but it requires a mutual commitment of effort from doctor and patient. Continuity consists of a combination of factors, not all of which have to be present. There is a sense of being known and knowing each other. Doctors demonstrate responsibility for the patient. Continuity can be mediated by the strength of the social relationship, by record keeping, by the comprehensiveness of the care given by an individual or a team, and by availability round the clock or in the patient's home.

There is plenty of evidence that doctors and patients value continuity, and some evidence that high continuity has a positive effect on some processes of care such as referral for tests. There is almost no evidence of the effectiveness of continuity on health outcomes. In fact there is anecdotal evidence that when a patient is familiar to a doctor, serious diagnoses are missed or delayed.

Conclusion

In our health care system, primary care organised around general practices with registered populations provides most people with most of their health care for most of the time.

There will continue to be a role for the primary care service in providing personalised care for people in their familiar surroundings, at low cost and relatively low risk. There are roles in personal health care for the sorter, advocate, gatekeeper, witness bearer, advisor and coach. There are the tasks of explanation, validation, diagnosis, prognosis and treatment. How these are organised and who provides them is up for discussion.

References

1. Morrell DC. *Diagnosis in general practice. Art or Science?* London: Nuffield Provincial Hospitals Trust, 1993.

2. Royal College of GPs. *The nature of general medical practice.* Report from General Practice No. 27. London: RCGP, 1995.

3. McWhinney IR. *A Textbook of Family Medicine.* 2nd ed. New York: OUP, 1997: Chapter 2, 13–29.

4. Department of Health. *Primary Care: Delivering the Future.* London: HMSO, 1996.

5. Department of Health. *The New NHS: modern, dependable.* London: HMSO, 1997.

6. Starfield B. *Primary Care. Concept, evaluation and policy.* Oxford: OUP, 1992.

7. Porter R. *The greatest benefit to mankind. A medical history of humanity from antiquity to the present.* London: HarperCollins, 1997.

8. McWhinney IR. A *Textbook of Family Medicine.* 2nd ed. New York: OUP, 1997: Chapter 1, 3–12.

9. Balint M *et al. Treatment or diagnosis? A study of repeat prescriptions in general practice.* London: Tavistock Publications, 1970.

10. Elwyn G, Edwards A and Kinnersley P. Shared decision-making in primary care: The neglected second half of the consultation. *British Journal of General Practice* 1999; 49: 441–45.

11. Summerton N. The medicine of primary care. *British Journal of General Practice* 1999; 49: 604–05.

12. Kernick DP. Nurses and doctors in primary care: decisions should be based on maximising the cost-effectiveness of a system of primary care and not the dictates of historical precedent. *British Journal of General Practice* 1999; 49: 647–49.

Chapter 10

Professional issues

Cyril Chantler

Professions

The case studies provoke questions concerning what should be done to help patients, who should do it and the rights of patients to decide. Such questions raise professional issues concerning the role of doctors and other health professionals and, within each profession, the roles of different practitioners such as general practitioners and consultants.

Professions exist to provide practitioners with mutual support, to provide training and education and to develop and maintain standards of practice. In a free market, mutual support may lead to the formation of a professional body acting to develop and maintain standards but it may also be concerned with matters which affect their financial status, hence George Bernard Shaw's aphorism that 'all professions are a conspiracy against the laity'.

Patients' needs

Standards set by professions are designed to protect the public not just from unqualified practitioners but also from the moral hazard of members of the profession unconsciously putting personal gain before the patient's interest when working in a free market. In the National Health Service there is another hazard. This is perhaps best appreciated by the observation that in the private sector surgeons are paid to operate, whereas in the NHS they are paid not to operate. Where the state pays, the doctor is partly freed from the obligation to satisfy patients' wants in order to maintain income. Here the moral hazard is that the patients' perspective will be disregarded and the professionals' view of patients' needs will be paramount.

Trust

Society and patients are less dependent on and trustful of professionals than they were at the start of the NHS. The information revolution has provided easy access to informed medical opinion without necessarily involving the patient's own doctor. Some treatments are of marginal benefit and carry considerable risks, and when things go wrong and are widely reported then patients' confidence and trust in their own doctors is undermined. We need to consider how to maintain or create trust in the light of these changes.

Consent

There is an increasing appreciation of the need to respect the autonomy of patients.[1] This has also led to widespread acceptance of the need to refine the doctor-patient relationship as a partnership where the health professional acts as an adviser and leaves it to the patient to determine what should be done after having received full information.[2] The case studies raise issues concerning informed consent and whether it is always appropriate that the doctor provides the necessary advice. Are there not circumstances where the nurse or another health professional has a better perspective? If so, how is this to be recognised and how is advice to be co-ordinated and provided?

Integrated care and 24-hour provision

The case of Father John not only raises issues concerning patient autonomy and the nature of consent, it also demonstrates clearly and tragically the problem of fragmentation in the delivery of care and communication failures that are all too common, particularly in the inner city. It is no exaggeration to say that in the evenings, at weekends and during holidays, anyone who is acutely unwell has a choice between visiting the local A&E department (often inappropriately) or calling one of the emergency GP locum services. Either way, the doctor who sees the patient will not have access to the case notes or be aware of the patient's previous history or agreed treatment plans. If the patient is acutely ill and sent to hospital, quite often treatment will have been instigated by the resident medical staff by the time the necessary information becomes available. Then, as in Father John's case, once the treatment has started, no matter how inappropriate, it is sometimes difficult to withdraw. A recent survey in Dundee showed that around 20 per cent of acute admissions were considered inappropriate when reviewed by the consultant physician on the next take-in ward round.[3] It is necessary to consider how these problems can be ameliorated and what the implications might be for the work of the different professionals in effecting whatever changes are proposed.

Who does what and who is responsible?

The case studies also suggest that it is not clear who should do what in providing care and treatment. It may be that tasks considered appropriate to one profession should be shared with or even undertaken by members of another profession to improve the effectiveness and efficiency of health care delivery. Changing the role of members of one profession may well affect the role of other professions and indeed provide a threat to their integrity. For example, expansion of the role of nurses and pharmacists may affect the responsibilities and status of doctors. We shall need to consider how to effect these changes and what is the role of education and regulation in promoting and sustaining such changes. Similar issues occur within a profession. For example, as consultants working in hospital become more and more specialised, so a vacuum is being created by the absence of those able to fulfil the role of general physician, surgeon or paediatrician.

If it is accepted that the essential responsibility of the doctor is to determine diagnosis – in other words, to answer the questions '*what is wrong?*' and '*why is it wrong?*' from a biomedical, psychological and social perspective – then the purely differentiated organ specialist is often unable to fulfil this role. Increasingly, the holistic, diagnostic role, as well as the treatment role, is the responsibility of the general practitioner. Unfortunately, however, it is difficult for general practitioners to maintain mastery of the broad range of diagnostic information and skills that are necessary, while participating fully in the provision of care and the provision of treatment. Therefore it may be that new divisions and sharing of responsibilities will be necessary within a multi-professional team. Certainly, the development of National Service Frameworks, and the realisation that much clinical activity relates to the chronically sick and disabled, means that better integration of hospital, primary care and community services is imperative. The failure of this integration is all too apparent in the case studies.

Problems with teams

The concept of teamwork is easy but too often the result is that no one knows the full picture, no one is in charge and no one is responsible. Even within a single profession the roles can be confused and the training and professional development haphazard. How can we ensure that younger doctors are supported and when dysfunction arises that those who act to deal with it are protected?

A new way?

This analysis might lead to the development of the concept of specialists working in highly-specialised semi-autonomous units in hospital, but who are nonetheless integrated into the community by working alongside general practitioners, particularly in a diagnostic and advisory role. General practitioners might themselves specialise more as general physicians or with a narrower specialty interest such as paediatrics, surgery or a disease specialty such as diabetes or rheumatology. They too could work as members of teams but would be community-based, though able to operate across their divide into the specialist units in hospitals. Each patient could have their own case adviser, not necessarily a doctor, to whom they could turn for advice. Necessarily, the development of doctors in this way would affect the policies of some of their institutions, such as the Royal Colleges or professional associations, and these will need to be discussed.

References

1. Chantler C. Reinventing Doctors. *BMJ* 1998; 317: 1670.

2. General Medical Council. *Seeking Patients' Consent: the ethical considerations*. London: GMC, 1999.

3. Duffy RJ. Personal communication.

Chapter 11

The implications for medical education

Roger Jones

Reforming medical education

In this chapter I will consider the ways in which medical education needs to change to deliver health care professionals for the 21st century. In doing so, I will attempt to make an explicit evaluation of the adequacies of recommendations made in 1993 by the General Medical Council (GMC) in *Tomorrow's Doctors*,[1] as well as the extent to which these recommendations have been implemented in medical school curricula in the UK.

By the late 1980s, medical education had evidently come a long way since the Todd[2] and Merrison reports[3] on the need for educational reform in medicine, but progress was patchy. Examples of good practice often existed cheek by jowl with painfully amateurish attempts at teaching medical students. *Tomorrow's Doctors* may have come as a surprise for some, but did not go far enough for others. Its key recommendations included a reduction in the factual content of the taught curriculum by around 25 per cent and balancing this by the provision of special study modules or options which students could take in health-related and other subjects. There was a strong emphasis on the explicit teaching and examination of communication and consulting skills and on the experience of medicine outside the hospital in primary care and community settings. In future teachers will have to be taught how to teach, and not merely to replicate the ways in which they were taught.

As the quality assessment of teaching (QAA) works through the medical schools we will learn more about the successes and failures of *Tomorrow's Doctors*. However, the case histories presented in this book give rise to other concerns, which we believe need to be addressed as medical education develops in the years ahead. These are expressed as ten questions for discussion:

The theoretical base of medical education – are the ingredients and balance right?

Traditional medical curricula interpreted basic sciences as anatomy, physiology, biochemistry and one or two other 'life sciences'. It has become clear that medicine demands major contributions from other 'basic' sciences, including medical sociology, health psychology, epidemiology and others such as medical ethics, which now comprises an early, taught course in many schools. Together these subjects form the thin end of the wedge of clinically-related material taught to new entrants to medical schools. The problems generated by the cases that we have read today emphasise the importance of the explicit incorporation of these subjects in the medical curricula, and of giving them weight comparable to the traditional biomedical and clinical sciences.

Father John's awful death throws up stark questions about the limits of medical interventions, the importance of understanding patients' views and shared decision-making, issues which are generalised to confront problems of rationing and responsibility in the case of Chris Adams. The important issues of end-of-life decision-making, living wills and advance directives need to be understood by undergraduates and postgraduates alike. Rationing and the use and costs of high-tech medical interventions are also important topics in the undergraduate curriculum. Undergraduate medical students need to understand that the complex interactions between people, medicine, society and themselves lie at the heart of many of these dilemmas, rather than seeing the behavioural sciences as 'add-ons' to biomedical and clinical rationalisations.

Communication skills – lip service or core?

Every one of the cases turns, at some point, on a communication problem; for instance, Ivy Brown and her difficult-to-reach ageing general practitioner, and Father John's inability to get through to and be taken seriously by his medical carers. *Tomorrow's Doctors* emphasised the importance of explicitly teaching and examining communication skills. Although schools are trying hard to do this by the use of role play, actors, objective structured clinical examinations (OSCEs) and other innovative approaches to teaching, learning and assessment, the importance of this thread of the curriculum is lost on many senior teachers and clinicians. 'Stick with me, my boy, and you'll learn everything you need to know about communication' is the communication skills analogue of the clinical apprenticeship, guaranteeing stagnation. Headline communication skills topics include patient-centredness, risk communication and obtaining informed consent. Concordance between doctors and patients – that is, a shared understanding of medical problems and their solutions – lies at the heart of effective patient management.

Medical schools and university hospitals – are research and teaching equally valued?

The immediate answer to this is 'no', if only because of the financial implications of the RAE (Research Assessment Exercise) compared with the QAA; of course, things may change.* The more considered answer is probably still 'no', and the reasons for this follow on from the two questions posed above. For academic staff in medical schools,

---

*Higher education establishments are assessed on the quality of their research (the RAE). They receive ratings which determine the amount of core funding they receive from the Higher Education Funding Council. The QAA looks at the performance management of teaching and its administration. The results have no effect on funding, which is based on student numbers. The GMC also inspects medical schools but has few sanctions against those who have not implemented their recommendations on curriculum reform.

progress and kudos are still largely research-related. Medical educational research remains at a primitive level and postgraduate professional advancement is strongly linked to research activity rather than teaching achievement. Perhaps a QAA with teeth will force the necessary rethinking of priorities in medical schools whose job, after all, is to teach medical students.

Finding evidence and getting it into practice – is this part of the curriculum?

This is an open question, whose answer will probably differ in different teaching settings. Ivy Brown's younger general practitioner may have been suffering from an excess of zeal, but in a number of the other cases management based on habit and anecdote, expediency and pragmatism seems to have taken the place of decisions based on appraisal of the best evidence. While recognising the limitations of evidence-based medicine, the importance of evidence in the determination of clinical effectiveness and the setting of standards for clinical governance should not be underestimated. This approach to clinical decision-making and management needs to be seen by our students as an explicit thread in their teaching and learning. Perhaps the most difficult challenge is to ensure that dangerous and useless practices are abandoned as new and effective ones are taken up.

Intellectual curiosity – is it alive in our medical schools?

This is another side of the previous question that has to be asked in relation to the curriculum changes that are now becoming widespread, including the move towards a core curriculum with special study modules (SSMs). The GMC's education committee obviously thought that the old curricula were turning out worn-out students, whose bright eyes and intellectual vigour dimmed as the course ground on. To some extent this is reflected in the unimaginative management approaches taken in some of the cases presented here, particularly Father John and Mary Fisher, but we have to be sure that the new curricula are not brewing up a baby-bathwater problem. As core curricula become more prescriptive, and the place of SSMs more clearly defined, we may be in danger of creating even more reductionist syllabuses in which the scope, on the part of both teachers and students, for lateral thinking, creativity and fun, is substantially reduced. This possibility represents a stern test of the delivery and assessment of new, highly structured and integrated curricula.

Managing ourselves and others – is this being taught?

The importance of integrated patient management, teamwork and delegation is highlighted by many of these case histories. Ivy Brown's GPs seem to have done her a disservice, which might have been prevented if they had worked better as a team. The importance of team care is highlighted in many of these cases and the high-cost examples emphasise the importance of management in a broader, population context. How much management should our students know about? They should certainly know how to look after themselves and manage their own time, to work with others, to share decisions and to delegate where appropriate. Little of this currently appears in medical school curricula, despite its self-evident importance in shaping a future where people with different approaches are able to work together.

Pastoral care – do we care and are we kind?

Again this follows on from questions about management. Recruitment and retention, as well as morale, remain problems in general practice and hospital medicine. Issues of self-regulation, clinical governance and revalidation lie behind the tragic stories that make the news headlines. Many of these cases emphasise the importance of producing new entrants to medicine in a professional environment which is caring and nutritive, rather than punitive and defensive, ensuring that they are able to retain their humanity while delivering medical care in a challenging multi-ethnic society.

The long-term relationships forged between GPs and their patients, and the understanding of the psychological and social background that comes with them, are likely to have lain at the cornerstone of cost-effective primary care in the UK. As we provide ever greater and faster access to medical services, via NHS Direct, walk-in centres at railway termini and over the Internet, we may pay a high price if continuity of care and personal medical care are seriously eroded.

What sort of doctor do we want? Do we know?

The GMC document emphasises the importance of bringing together knowledge, skills and attitudes in considering the qualities of a doctor, and our case histories emphasise the multifaceted nature of the medical task and the importance of balancing skills, knowledge and the range of attitudes that are taught and absorbed during training and beyond. In a way this question is a distillation of all the previous ones; would a different kind of doctor have made different kinds of decisions in the face of the very difficult problems posed by our patients, particularly Father John and Mary Fisher? What sort of doctor do we need to take the public health decisions in which high costs and rationing are central features? Have medical schools thought long enough and hard enough about this, and even if they have how on earth do we make sure that our graduates measure up to our aspirations?

Student selection – have we got it right?

This is the 'input' side of the previous question: what sort of students do we need to produce the kind of doctors that we think we want? As we move down this list of questions, the evidence on which to base their answers seems to become more and more scanty. More research is required to define student entry criteria in relation to the kind of graduates that we think we will need to deliver medical care in the 21st century.

Continuing medical education – lifelong learning or form filling?

Beyond the medical school, for 30 or 40 years there are many demands on doctors. They need to stay up-to-date, remain fresh and interested, kind and caring, retain their imagination and sense of humour and demonstrate to their peers and the public that they are still fit to practise in their chosen field of medicine. This is an immensely tall order, and continuing medical education still wrestles with the challenge of providing relevant teaching throughout the lives of medical practitioners. Many doctors become harder and harder to reach as they age and, paradoxically, as medical education becomes more and more important for them. How can we find an appropriate way to ensure that revalidation and reaccreditation go hand-in-hand with continuing development rather than attempts at punishment?

Tomorrow's Doctors represented a brave start to the reform of medical education in the UK. However, the challenges posed by our case studies underline the persistence of a number of crucial questions about the aims of medical education and the methods that should be used to train medical graduates interested in responding to the challenges of medicine in the years to come.

References

1. General Medical Council. *Tomorrow's Doctors*. London: GMC, 1993.

2. Her Majesty's Stationery Office. *Report of the Royal Commission on Medical Education* (The Todd Report). London: HMSO, 1968.

3. Her Majesty's Stationery Office. *Report of the Royal Commission on the National Health Service* (The Merrison Report). London: HMSO, 1979.

Chapter 12

Four challenges for NHS policy-makers

Angela Coulter

Introduction

The UK spends less on health care than most of its European partners. Health spending is considerably higher in Germany, France, The Netherlands, Austria, Switzerland, Spain, Sweden, Norway, Italy and Finland. In a comparison of health spending in 29 OECD countries only Turkey, Poland, Mexico and Korea spent a lower proportion of their gross domestic product (GDP) on health care.[1] The UK's spending in 1997 was 6.7 per cent of GDP as against the OECD average of 7.5 per cent. In per capita terms, the UK spent US \$1347 per head of population compared to Germany's \$2339 and \$2051 in France.

The NHS can, with some justification, claim to be more efficient than the health systems in many of these other countries. For example, in 1992 average lengths of stay were shortest in the UK at 5.5 days compared to Germany's average of 12.6 days.[2] The relatively well-organised general practice gatekeeper system is another reason why the UK manages to hold costs down,[3] but in other respects it is now clear that the UK is lagging behind comparable countries. Deaths from coronary heart disease are among the highest in Europe, cancer survival rates are relatively poor and we have a particularly high rate of teenage pregnancies. Many hospital buildings are substandard, standards in general practice and community nursing are highly variable, and low pay and poor working conditions are leading to recruitment difficulties, particularly among nurses and some medical specialties.

Despite the evidence of deficiencies, the NHS continues to attract considerable public support. Dissatisfaction with the service has increased over the past 15 years, but in surveys the majority of respondents report high levels of satisfaction, especially with primary care.[4] The British public appears to be willing to contemplate paying more for their health care. In 1996, 54 per cent of a random population sample named health as their first priority for extra government spending and 59 per cent said the Government should increase taxes and spend more. But despite the apparent willingness to sanction increased taxes the electorate tends to shy away from this commitment at election times, leading to tight caps on NHS spending. Meanwhile rising public expectations, demographic change and the high cost of new technological developments are placing the service under increased pressure.

As yet there has not been a mass exodus to the private sector, but doubt remains about the fortitude of the post-war consensus on welfare. How much longer will people tolerate low standards of comfort, privacy and responsiveness? Can the NHS modernise itself? The five case studies outlined in this book illustrate different aspects of the 'system stress' that currently afflicts the service. Drawing on these examples I shall briefly outline four key challenges that face policy-makers if the NHS is to survive well into the new millennium.

How to ensure that all patients receive high quality clinical care?

The patients in the case studies seem a remarkably uncomplaining bunch, but each suffered from poor quality of care when looked at from their point of view. Ivy Brown's GP showed little interest in her problem; Father John suffered interventions that were inappropriate to his needs and wishes; busy hospital staff completely failed to cope with Mary Fisher's physical and emotional needs; and Luke Warm Luke failed to find appropriate support and crisis intervention when he needed it, with the result that his condition deteriorated alarmingly.

In its response to the growing evidence of system failures the Government is setting considerable store by the new mechanisms it has established to root out problems and raise standards of clinical care. The National Institute for Clinical Excellence (NICE) and the National Service Frameworks will set national quality standards; the Commission for Health Improvement (CHI), the national performance framework and the national patient and user survey will monitor performance against these standards; and trusts will be expected to engage all staff in quality improvement through the new system of clinical governance.

The problem with formal systems for monitoring quality is that they can easily fall into the trap of measuring the easily measurable and ignoring the less tangible but often more important aspects of health care. It will be a tough challenge to devise a system that could eliminate the bad experiences of the patients in our case studies. There is a natural tendency to look for scapegoats when evidence of bad practice emerges, but quality failures can rarely be pinpointed to the action of a few individuals. More often they are the result of a system failure in which processes to assure quality were not in place or were not working properly. A system failure requires a system-wide solution. Is it better to rely on centrally directed, coercive approaches to quality improvement, or will bottom-up facultative approaches which rely on staff involvement and personal commitment be more successful? Quality may not be best served by a climate of fear, but methods that depend on voluntary involvement can be ignored by those whose practices give most cause for concern. It seems likely that a combination of carrot and stick is required, but what is the optimal balance?

How to deliver a seamless service?

When Ivy Brown was admitted to hospital no one bothered to keep her GP informed of what was going on. Mary Fisher's discharge from hospital was unco-ordinated and chaotic, her GP and the district nurse did not communicate adequately and she received very little support at home. Not surprisingly her health deteriorated further. Luke Warm Luke had contact with a wide range of services, including school, police, courts, prison, probation, social work, general practice, psychiatry, ambulance and housing, but the large number of professionals who had some input into his care collectively failed to provide timely and appropriate support, which might have prevented the downward spiral. Intervention and support at school might have given him a better start in life, earlier diagnosis might have diverted him from prison, an assertive outreach team could have gone to find him when he failed to attend medical appointments, 24-hour crisis centres might have been able to calm him when he was feeling violent. Above all, he needed someone to take an interest in him, to help him co-ordinate his journey between these different agencies, to listen to and learn from his views and preferences, and to alert key people when things were going wrong.

Unfortunately these experiences are all too common. Despite multiple Government pronouncements, numerous working parties and joint planning meetings and good intentions all round, co-ordination and team work across professional and service boundaries is still a major weakness in the system. It is also a major cause of inefficiency and inappropriate use of resources. Many of the problems suffered by these people could have been avoided if their care had been better co-ordinated, if professionals had communicated better and if people had acted proactively before problems developed instead of waiting until there was a crisis.

What is at the root of this failure? Is it the inevitable result of underfunding or is there another preventable cause? Is the answer to be found in the structure, organisation or funding of services, or would better training solve the problem? What incentives could be introduced to encourage staff to set aside professional rivalries and see things from the patient's point of view? Is there anything to be learned from other sectors of the economy – industry or business for example – which would assist in the development of better co-ordination between health, social services and other agencies providing basic needs such as housing and social security? What should the Government do to turn its partnership rhetoric into reality?

How to promote self-help and reduce dependence?

A strong thread of paternalism runs through our case studies, illustrating one of the NHS's most besetting problems. Paternalist attitudes are damaging to recovery because they deny patients' autonomy, creating dependency on professionals and undermining people's confidence to deal with their own problems. Ivy Brown, Mary Fisher and Chris Adams were left without adequate explanation of their health problems, the likely prognosis, or the treatment options. No one seemed to consider that their views and preferences were particularly important. The emergency services took decisions about Father John's care without bothering to find out what had been agreed between him and his regular doctor. Mary Fisher's day hospital did little to promote her independence and ability to cope on her own. Professionals seemed reluctant to share their uncertainties with their patients and as a result acted precipitately with inappropriate decisiveness based on inaccurate presumptions about their patients' wishes.

Attitudes among staff in the NHS often appear to be out of touch with wider social changes and public expectations. The rise of consumerism and the rapid development of access to electronic media and information systems are changing the way lay people think about professionals. The public is no longer willing to tolerate 'doctor knows best' attitudes. Instead they look for clear explanations and more involvement in decisions that affect them. Most people want to help themselves and to live independent lives if at all possible. Some of the caring services are especially guilty of promoting dependence. A patient or client-centred approach to the provision of day services which supported active rehabilitation in people's own homes and local communities might look very different from the dependency-creating institution where Mary Fisher ended up. People are no longer willing to tolerate the indignities of mixed wards, long waits in out-patients to receive brisk treatment from distracted doctors, and lack of choice or respect for their views and preferences. Unless the NHS comes to grips with the culture change and turns it to best advantage, public support for a national service will wither away.

What is to be done? There is clearly a need for more and better training in communication skills, but stronger measures will be required if the system is to adapt. The organisational culture needs to shift towards a truly patient-centred approach. Individual preferences, and differences, will have to be accorded much greater respect. Services must become more flexible. Staff must be empowered to think creatively. User involvement must be encouraged at all levels of the service – at the individual level in discussions between clinicians and patients, at the level of service design and evaluation, and in debates about health priorities. But this poses a potentially threatening challenge to health professionals. How can they be helped to adapt? What support will they need if they are to be encouraged to forgo some of their autonomy and pay greater attention to the views of patients and their advocates? What practical steps can be taken to meet patients' information needs? What scope is there to offer patients more choice? Is choice compatible with equity, a fundamental NHS value? Is there a danger that consumer demands will outstrip the capacity of the NHS to deliver?

How to make hard choices between competing priorities?

Politicians frequently deny the existence of rationing in the NHS, but it is and always has been a feature of health care delivery in every country. Rationing is the process of choosing which beneficial services should be offered to whom, and which should not. If the NHS had access to unlimited resources rationing would not be an issue, but a service which has to operate within budget limits cannot avoid the need to make hard choices.

These hard choices were very evident in Chris Adams' case. The health authority tried to weigh up the costs of his care against the benefits that would have to be foregone by other patients for whom they were responsible once their budget was spent. This was a stark choice, which they attempted to deal with in an explicit and rational manner. But rationing was also a feature of the care of the other patients described in the case studies, albeit implicitly. Mary Fisher was affected by rationing because community services in her area were inadequate to meet her needs, presumably because her health authority had given these lower priority than the other demands on its resources. Luke Warm Luke was not offered alternatives to chlorpromazine despite his dislike of the unpleasant side effects, possibly because the alternatives were considered too expensive. Ivy Brown's relatives managed to persuade the doctors to prolong her treatment in intensive care despite the fact that this must have consumed resources which might have been spent on patients with greater chance of benefit.

In establishing the National Institute for Clinical Excellence the Government has acknowledged the need for a more rational and transparent mechanism for deciding on priorities, but this process cannot be value-free. Decisions about the allocation of health care resources can, and should, be based on sound evidence about the potential benefit derived from particular treatments and the cost of providing them. But making these choices depends on values as well as technical evidence. The decision about whether or not to allocate resources to a particular treatment or service involves consideration of whether it is affordable in relation to other calls on funds, and whether it is an appropriate use of taxpayers' money. 'Rational' rationing requires a consensus on the objectives and scope of the NHS (for example, is it appropriate for a public service to treat impotence or infertility?) and on the desired outcomes of medical treatment. There has to be agreement on the relative importance of the various goals of the service and on how its performance should be measured. And in making choices between competing demands on resources one has to decide whose values should be taken into account (the public, patients, carers, user groups, clinicians, managers, politicians?) and who should be the final arbiter when these values conflict.

However much the Government may want to present the appraisal of new treatments and technologies as a purely technical process to be consigned to expert committees, it is clear that decisions about affordability and appropriateness are political issues which should be open to public scrutiny and debate. In Chris Adams' case, the health authority tried to examine the evidence and debate the issue rationally, only to find that their hands were tied legally. The lawyers advised that the individual patient's needs had to take precedence because it was hard to quantify the benefits likely to be foregone by other patients. In other cases like this, health authorities have found it difficult to resist legal challenge to their decisions. They are also vulnerable to adverse publicity in the media and public protests. Their vulnerability is in part due to the lack of local democratic accountability in the health service. As government-appointed bodies their legitimacy is derived from their position in the NHS hierarchy, but ministers keep them at arms length, denying the very existence of rationing in the health service, providing little support for their tough decisions but hauling them over the coals when they overspend their budgets.

What can be done to put an end to this hypocrisy? Is NICE the answer? What processes could be put in place to educate the public about the choices that need to be faced and to involve them in the key policy decisions? Should health authorities become bodies of elected representatives? Would this make decision-making more or less difficult? How would it square with the shift to primary care-led purchasing with GPs in the driving seat? Should clinicians be more aware of budgetary considerations when making treatment decisions? Should patients and their relatives be told about the cost of their treatment?

There are no easy answers to these dilemmas, but if the NHS is to survive its supporters will need to ensure that the contradictions and problems are not just swept under the carpet. They will have to be faced in an open and transparent manner and the British public will have to remain convinced that this method of organising and paying for health care continues to be preferable to the alternatives.

References

1.   OECD Health Data 98. *A comparative analysis of twenty-nine countries.* Paris: Organization for Economic Co-operation and Development, 1998.

2.   Rosieff F and Lister G. *European healthcare trends: towards managed care in Europe.* Coopers and Lybrand Europe Ltd, 1995.

3.   Starfield B. Is primary care essential? *Lancet* 1994; 344: 1129–33.

4.   Mulligan J. Attitudes towards the NHS and its alternatives, 1983–96. *Health Care UK 1997/98.* London: King's Fund, 1998: 198–209.

Part 3

What should be done?

Chapter 13

The conclusions and recommendations of the Leeds Castle Foundation medical conference*

Background

Health care, we know, can go disastrously wrong. This is not just a matter of incompetent practitioners causing injury to patients through negligence or misconduct. The bigger issue is 'system failure' – the failure of the NHS to deliver the standard of care patients have a right to expect. As medicine becomes more complex, the opportunities for failure have increased. Often the question is not what can be done but what should be done.

The cases considered demonstrate the cruelty and the inhumanity of which the NHS is capable. Yet all the staff were doing their best and their relatives would be hard pressed to make a charge of negligence or incompetence stick. What these cases demonstrate is the powerlessness of patients in a health service that denies choice and is dominated by a paternalistic ethic. The cases show how patient's choices were ignored

---

*How should the delivery of health care be organised to meet patients' and society's needs in the NHS? Edited extract from the Report of the Leeds Castle Foundation medical conference, 24–26 October 1999, *Health Challenges beyond the Year 2000*. Reproduced by kind permission of the Leeds Castle Foundation and Sir Roger Bannister, Medical Trustee. The conclusions and recommendations in this chapter were agreed by participants who attended the event on 24–26 October. A list of members is included at the end of the chapter.

(Father John), they were not heard (Ivy Brown and Luke Warm Luke), or they could not understand what was going on.

The terms of reference of the conference were to examine health care as it is now funded and to propose improvements.

Possible strategies

Empowering patients

A key theme that emerged was the need to empower patients and increase their choice about what happens to them. A radical strategy is required to shift the balance of power from the doctor to patient. Such a shift is vital if the NHS is to retain the public support necessary to survive the pressures it will come under in the 21st century.

Traditionally the NHS had been professionally dominated rather than patient-centred. Increasingly, however, the utilitarian principle of achieving the greatest good for the greatest number on which it was founded is being challenged by a rights-based model that highlights the importance of citizenship. The lack of choice leaves younger people, in particular, less attached to the NHS than older people. It must become more patient focused.

This is important medically, to improve care, and politically, to maintain support for the NHS as a publicly-funded health care system. Evidence suggests that patients want to play a part in managing their care and that when they do, they get better quicker and are more satisfied with their care.

Supporting choice

The complexity of modern health care means that patients need to take more control. Choice is determined by professionals, not patients – paternalism is the besetting sin of the NHS. Lack of choice and control are unlikely to go on being acceptable.

Some patients may not want greater choice. They expect the doctor to decide what's best. Should their wishes be respected?

The majority of the group felt the answer had to be 'no'. Choosing to remain in deferential mode is no longer a tenable position in a modern health service. Giving informed consent requires an understanding of the treatment proposed. If patients give informed consent, one way or another that throws back responsibility on them. It is a multi-staged process that may involve long-term negotiation.

Extending knowledge

It is sometimes argued that giving patients extra choice means extra cost because it implies surplus. But this is not so. Medical treatments tend to be oversold by those trained to deliver them. The quantity of pills flushed down the lavatory is the price of paternalism. Surgeons trained in particular skills have to be optimistic about their outcome.

Patients need to be trained to assess medical risks and probabilities and to find other sources of information, as they already do as ordinary consumers. Watching and waiting may be preferable to treatment. Giving patients choice does not necessarily mean giving more treatment.

As sources of information and advice proliferate, we need to think of the health system as a knowledge system. Doctors know where to go for the best advice. Why should not the rest of the population have that advantage?

Improving communication

There is a view that medicine has lost touch with its soul – it has got the science right but has lost its humanity. There is sometimes an almost necessary impersonal streak in medical education. Treating the NHS as a machine distances its staff and its patients. Kindness is part of care.

Delivering teamwork

Teamwork is now accepted as fundamental to good health care but it is failing to deliver. The chief problem is that no one is in charge and knows the full picture. Patients fall through the gaps. Integration, co-ordination and better organisation are key. Policy-makers, however, tend to be uninterested in breaking down (service) boundaries, such as between primary and secondary care, because they are a way of restricting demand.

Encouraging autonomy

One of the aims of medical care must be to encourage patients to take more responsibility for themselves, by increasing their autonomy. The NHS as it is currently organised encourages dependence. This has to change.

The proposals

At the patient level – patient-held records

A simple but radical step towards solving these problems would be to give patients their own medical records to hold. The aim would be to provide patients with a summary of their GP notes together with copies of their hospital referral letters and any care plans or advanced directives. The information they contained would be less important than the impact on patient and professional attitudes. The principle of placing information in the patient's hands is seen as key to shifting control.

With advanced technology, the record could in time be developed as a smart medical card or electronic medical summary record. Later a 'smarter' card giving the patient access to relevant information over the Internet might be developed. Ultimately a patient's individual genetic makeup might be carried on the smart card, helping target effective treatment and reducing idiosyncratic side effects. Prescribing would be unthinkable without it.

The idea of patients holding their own records is not new. Where patient-held records have been tried, experience shows that their owners look after them better than the NHS. They tend, however, to provoke turf wars among professionals over the format of the records and what should go in them.

A key worker and a care plan

Patients will however, need help to make use of the information. A key worker should be available to anyone who requests one, to guide them round the system, to oversee their care plan and to see that it is carried out. In this context, thought needs to be given to the changing roles of professionals as 'enablers'. The aim would be to improve communication, continuity and co-ordination.

Training and public education

To help patients make the necessary cultural shift involved in taking control of their records, training and public education would need to be provided to win their acceptance and to furnish them with the necessary skills to negotiate the health care system. This would also provide an opportunity to pursue a wider public health agenda, promoting key messages. Television could be enlisted for educational programmes.

A competitive market in health advisers is already developing. There are possibilities of public–private partnerships in this field.

At the organisational level – the intermediate integrated health centre

In the modern NHS, 80 per cent of clinical activity relates to the chronically sick and disabled. As care has become more complex so it has become more fragmented. Better integration of hospital, primary care and community service is imperative.

The intermediate health care centre is aimed at bridging the primary-secondary-local authority divide. It should be piloted in inner city areas. The aim would be to build on the demand for walk-in services, link that with traditional GP services providing continuity of care and also offer social and voluntary services and, possibly, beds for elderly people.

The development would link with the trend to fewer, larger scale hospitals that create problems of access, by meeting the need for more basic hospital services nearer home.

Teamworking and skilled leadership

Teamworking needs to be strengthened by identifying a skilled leader and clarifying roles and responsibilities of each team member. Teams also need realistic job plans and two-way appraisal (doctors and managers appraising each other) to improve understanding between clinicians and managers. Local flexibility must be built in to allow teams to find local solutions to constraints on the service that make them appear over-bureaucratised and uncaring. This is seen as a way of giving staff greater control over their working lives and improving morale.

At national level – define the scope of the NHS

An explicit policy must be developed charting the scope of the NHS and setting out what it will and will not fund. A public debate is needed about how far the NHS should move from a needs-based to a rights-based service. One of the issues is whether an element of co-payment should be introduced to expand the range of choices on offer to patients. Co-payment could be introduced for patients who request a second opinion within the NHS.

Finding ways of communicating risk to patients

There is a need for a new research and development programme on the communication of risk. More emphasis in publicly-funded research needs to be placed on questions of whether treatments work in real life, outside clinical trials, and whether they are worth it.

Support for multi-professional training

The regulatory bodies for doctors (GMC) and nurses (UKCC) should be asked to give their support to multi-professional training. The aim is to stimulate cross-disciplinary working, but agreement is needed on the core skills to be taught.

Raise the profile of teaching medical students

The funding of medical schools should be linked as much to teaching quality as to research success. There is a need to highlight teaching as the central role of medical schools and focus attention more closely on it.

Leeds Castle Foundation medical conference membership (job title as of October 1999)

Ms Amanda Beswick	Agency Initiatives Manager, Peabody Trust
Professor Tim Brighouse	Birmingham Chief Education Officer
Dr Harry Burns	Director of Public Health, Greater Glasgow Health Board
Professor Sir Cyril Chantler	Dean, Guy's, King's College and St Thomas' Hospitals' Medical and Dental School and Vice-Principal of King's College, London
Ms Anna Coote	Director, Public Health Programme, King's Fund
Dr Angela Coulter	Director, Policy & Development, King's Fund

Dr Deirdre Cunningham	Director, Health Policy & Public Health, Lambeth, Southwark & Lewisham
Ms Lucy Hamer	Transport Studies Group, University of Westminster
Ms Christine Hancock	General Secretary, Royal College of Nursing
Sir Graham Hart	Chairman, King's Fund
Dr Alison P Hill	Director, Effective Practice Programme, King's Fund
Dr Richard Horton	Editor-in-Chief, *The Lancet*
Mr James Johnson	Chairman, JCC (Professional Standards), BMA
Professor Roger Jones	Head, Department of General Practice & Primary Care, Guy's, King's College and St Thomas' Hospitals' Medical School
Mr Jeremy Laurance	Health Editor, *The Independent*
Professor Julian Le Grand	Professor, Social Policy, LSE
Mr Charles Leadbeater	Author
Ms Jo Lenaghan	Director of Health & Social Policy, IPPR
Ms Wilma McPherson	Director of Quality & Nursing, Guy's and St Thomas' Hospital Trust
Rabbi Julia Neuberger	Chief Executive, King's Fund
Mr John Wyn Owen	Secretary, The Nuffield Trust
Shushila Patel	Commission for Racial Equality

Dr David Percy   Director of Education & Training,
                                        South East NHS Executive

Mr Barry Quirk   Chief Executive, London Borough of
                                        Lewisham

Professor Sir Michael Rawlins   Chairman, National Institute for
                                        Clinical Excellence

Ms Imogen Sharp   Director, National Heart Forum

Professor Drew Stevenson   Professor of Urban Regeneration,
                                        University of London

Leeds Castle Foundation

Sir Roger Bannister   Medical Trustee

Mrs Pam Holdsworth   Conference Secretary

Chapter 14

Conclusion

Cyril Chantler

It is widely felt that anecdotes have no validity as evidence for the determination of policy for the delivery of health care. Quantitative methodology rules and even qualitative research often has to be quantified before it is acceptable. Unfortunately means and standard deviations cannot describe the totality of an individual's experience in the health service, and each individual's experience is different. As medical students come to realise, textbooks and teaching provide the vocabulary and grammar of medicine but they do not enable one to speak the language. The health system has to work for individuals in all circumstances and therefore case studies are important, as long as they are reasonably typical. We were particularly anxious to understand the problems before attempting to find solutions, to develop what has been called a 'rich question'.[1]

Having reached a consensus around the problem, the next task was to make practical suggestions that, if implemented, might improve the experience of those with similar problems in the future. The suggestions that resulted are not in any way comprehensive and they were certainly constrained deliberately by some of the disciplines that the group imposed on itself. We did not, for example, address the issue of public health or public health medicine, though we would all accept its importance. However, in our recommendations, we believe there are many opportunities to improve health education for individuals in the structures we proposed.

We assumed that public resources would rise within historical rates of increase, not because we thought that no more should be provided, but because we considered that even if we are able (as the Prime Minister hopes) to match the spending in other European countries, problems will still remain unless other actions are taken. We also felt that were we to include resource questions in our discussions, they would dominate and therefore prevent us addressing other issues. We did, however, suggest that a debate was required concerning whether more elements of co-payment might be desirable within the NHS, both to provide extra funds but also to provide more choice at the individual's discretion and to reduce moral hazard in the usage and provision of services. It is clear that the Government would not wish to implement the suggestion that we made regarding co-payment for patients who request a second opinion. But whatever systems are developed we nonetheless believe that choice is necessary and should be possible in the NHS, rather than requiring individuals to opt out of the NHS into the private sector. Choices encourage comparisons. Competition through comparison rather than competition through financial advantage is a legitimate and necessary way of improving standards. For this to be effective, the NHS requires accurate information concerning costs and outcomes so that choice can be exercised and a continuous cycle of learning and improvement can be established.

The introduction of National Service Frameworks means that there is a need to provide an integrated approach to the management of chronic diseases. This in turn requires teamwork, which necessarily involves the integration of services across the divide from the hospital to primary care and the community services. We also need integration with agencies outside the health service, such as social services, and the voluntary service. We need to see the integration of both the planning and delivery of health care with Health Improvement Programmes and Health Action Zones. Our proposals were formulated with the understanding that these changes were occurring and had to be accommodated.

We also recognised the complexity of care, both in terms of the technology and of the delivery systems in hospital and the community. So we recommend that each patient requires a care manager who can set out choices in an informed way, to which the patient can respond.

Such a key worker or care manager could also serve to integrate the care between the different agencies and between the different professionals within the service. In this respect, the increasing tendency for greater specialisation in the hospital secondary service leaves a gap between the super specialist and the general practitioner that needs to be filled. The involvement of general physicians or general paediatricians or general obstetricians, for example, operating between the community and the specialist service in hospital, might help to fill this medical gap.

We also recognised that the gap was widening between what can be done and what should be done, both in terms of what is financially affordable but also recognising that in some instances the provision of non-technological care might be a more appropriate intervention than high-tech treatment. Again, better information is required for patients to make these decisions for themselves.

Finally, we recognised that changing work patterns among health professionals, with shorter working hours and the removal of a 24-hour commitment, emphasised the need to develop teamwork to a high degree of efficiency and also the need to examine professional roles and the sharing of responsibilities.

Our suggestions, therefore, were designed to meet a number of challenges. It is perhaps important to emphasise that the proposals were not lineally related to the problems that were identified. Rather, both the problems and the solutions were integrated, therefore some suggestions will ameliorate more than one problem. We believe that our suggestions are manageable in the sense that each can be tested and analysed before being applied universally. Indeed, it may well be that different communities require different solutions.

The NHS of the new millennium needs to be a thoughtful, integrated, patient-aware organisation that runs on partnership and collaboration with all parts of the wider health system. We believe that the proposals presented in this book are realistic, based as they are on policy analysis and on case histories. We believe also that they are realistic in relation to the demands of the NHS at the present time. It remains to find the resources, capacity and determination to test them in action. We believe that these are to be found in today's NHS.

References

1. Heirs B. *The Professional Decision-Thinker and the Art of Team Thinking Leadership*. London: Grafton, 1989.

Contributors

Professor Sir Cyril Chantler, Chair
Dean of the Guy's, King's College and St Thomas' Hospitals' Medical and Dental School and Vice-Principal of King's College London. He is also the Children's Nationwide Medical Research Fund Professor of Paediatric Nephrology at Guy's. He is Pro Vice-Chancellor for Medicine, University of London and Chairman of the Conference of Metropolitan Deans. Chairman of the Standards Committee of the GMC.

Dr Angela Coulter
Chief Executive of the Picker Institute Europe. She is a Visiting Professor at the Royal Free and University College Schools of Medicine, a Visiting Fellow at Nuffield College, Oxford and a Governor of Oxford Brookes University. At the time of the Leeds Castle conference she was Director of Policy and Development at the King's Fund, London. She is the founding editor of Health Expectations.

Dr Deirdre Cunningham
Director of Public Health and Health Systems at Lambeth, Southwark and Lewisham Health Authority. She is also working to set up the London Health Observatory.

Professor Len Doyal
Professor of Medical Ethics in the Department of Human Science and Medical Ethics, St Bartholomew's and the Royal London School of Medicine and Dentistry, Queen Mary and Westfield College, London.

Dr Alison P Hill
Formerly Director of the Effective Practice Programme at the King's Fund. She is a GP who has held posts in health service management, medical education and research.

Professor Roger Jones
Wolfson Professor of General Practice, Guy's, King's and St Thomas' School of Medicine, London. He is President of the Primary Care Society for Gastroenterology, chairs the European Society for Primary Care Gastroenterology and is the Editor of *Family Practice*.